THOM ATKINS

Beading
Artistry
FOR QUILTS

Basic Stitches & Embellishments
Add Texture & Drama

C&T PUBLISHING

Text and Artwork copyright © 2012 by Thom Atkins

Photography and Artwork copyright
© 2012 by C&T Publishing, Inc.

Publisher: Amy Marson

Creative Director: Gailen Runge

Art Director: Kristy Zacharaias

Editor: Liz Aneloski

Technical Editors: Ann Haley and Gailen Runge

Cover/Book Designer: April Mostek

Production Coordinator: Jessica Jenkins

Production Editor: S. Michele Fry

Illustrator: Tim Manibusan

Photography by Christina Carty-Francis and Diane Pedersen
of C&T Publishing, Inc., unless otherwise noted

How-To Photography by Thom Atkins, unless otherwise noted

Published by C&T Publishing, Inc., P.O. Box 1456, Lafayette,
CA 94549

Library of Congress Cataloging-in-Publication Data

Atkins, Thom, 1944-

 Beading artistry for quilts : basic stitches and embellishments
add texture and drama / Thom Atkins.

  pages cm

ISBN: 978-1-60705-584-6 (soft cover)

1. Beadwork. 2. Quilting. I. Atkins, Thom, 1944- Works.
Selections. 2012. II. Title.

TT860.A85 2012

746.46--dc23

Printed in China

10 9 8 7 6 5 4 3 2 1

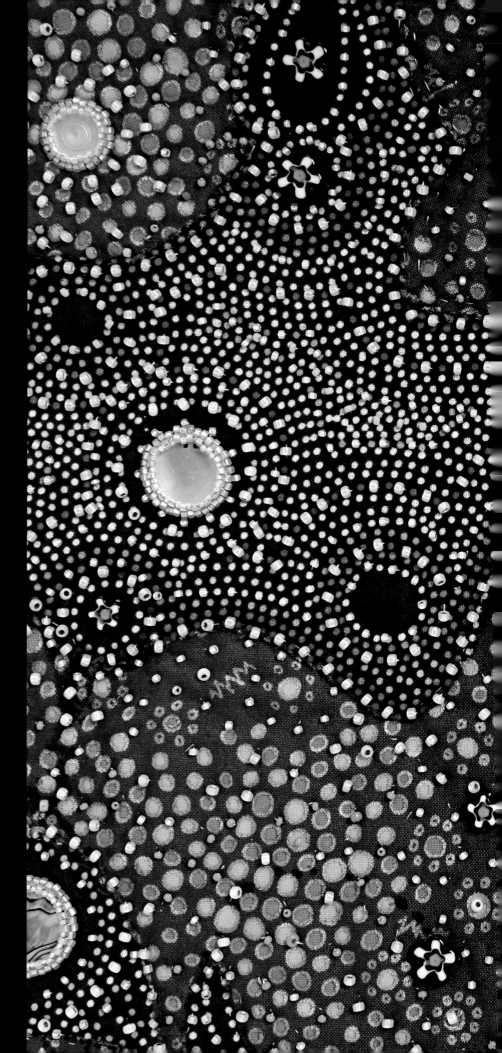

Dedication

I would like to dedicate this book to the four most important women in my life: my grandmother, Martha (Dede) Atkins; my mom, Ferne Cook; my sister, Robin Atkins; and my wife, Jennifer Chase, all of whom have had a hand in providing the tools to get me from this book's inception to the reality of print.

Acknowledgments

During the year and a half we stayed with my grandparents after my father's death, my grandmother taught my sister and me how to sew on a treadle sewing machine. This, for me, was the beginning of a long career of "sticking things together." My mom and stepfather both encouraged me to look at things from the perspective of "I don't know how to do that … yet!" rather than the usual "I CAN'T!" My sister, Robin, arrived in the world of beads by a whole different path and provided me with the basic stitches of bead embroidery, as well as a foundation of "off-loom weaving" techniques. My wife, Jennifer, has been a pillar of strength and support for all my artistic endeavors and is the one who provided a regular paycheck and health insurance so I could pursue less monetarily remunerative goals and provide us with "the pretty things." I would also like to thank the ladies at C&T Publishing, who thought I had a book to write long before I realized I had enough to say.

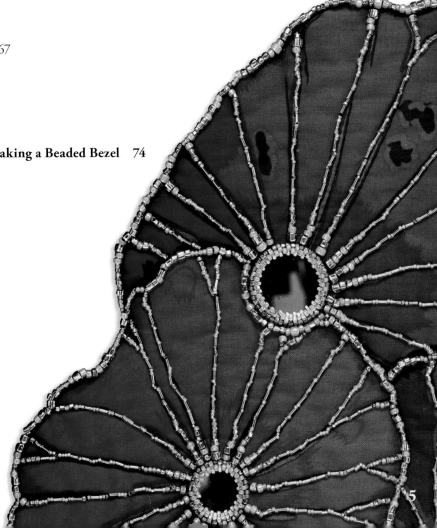

Introduction

Sewing beads onto quilts, for me, is a great deal more than just embellishment. My ultimate goal, for the past ten years or so, has been to find the balance between the fabric and the beads.

How I start a piece varies greatly. I may have a bolt of fabric leap off the shelf and scream, "Take me home!" I may see a particular bead or color of bead that sets me off, or I may have an image or idea I want to express. There are times when I start a piece and have no idea how I'm going to use beads on it, knowing only that I will use them somewhere, somehow. There are times when I want a particular effect, like falling rain, which can be done beautifully with beads. Then I design the piece with that in mind, the beads forming the focal point over and above the design happening in the fabric. If one were to look at all the work I've done in the past ten years, the most obvious continuity is in the use of the beads.

For me, my most valuable tool is the question, "What would happen if I … ?" Encountering new techniques, such as netting capture, boiling polyester organza to produce permanent shapes, reverse appliqué, and even felting, provides grist for my creativity. These techniques often furnish me with a way to actually say something, rather than just creating something "pretty." Once the technique has been explored, the fabric face created, the beads chosen, and beading patterns established, there comes a period of time where it is just the "donkey work" of finishing. Then, the beading becomes rather Zen-like, and I keep moving through what could be boring toward the goal of satisfying my curiosity, as I wonder, "What is it going to look like? Will it look anything like what I saw in my mind?"

My purpose in this book is to share not only the tools of "how to sew beads onto a quilt," but also a bit about the whys. Being a very visual person who has great difficulty reading and understanding directions, let alone following them, I had some—well, let's say a lot of—reservations about writing a book of instructions; I would rather have just given you a great many pictures and illustrations. Yet I find that the written word may help with understanding where the pictures fall short.

We each have our own ways of processing information and then using it to create something that is uniquely ours. Making the leap from constructing something someone else has designed to creating something on our own is huge. I hope the information and techniques you find in this book will help you do just that.

Why Use Beads on Your Quilts?

Why use beads on a quilt? I would as well ask you, why sing, why dance, why write poetry or paint paintings? I've been fascinated with beads ever since the early '70s when I managed a craft gallery and was gifted with some lovely African trade beads. I didn't know they were valuable then, only that they were beautiful. I took apart strands and made jewelry for myself and others. Later, I drilled holes in some shells I had gathered on Ocracoke Island, North Carolina, thereby making them into beads in the time-honored tradition. I still have a necklace from those shells, although I never wear it. But I digress. Beads do that to me.

Why quilt? Why sew together pieces of fabric to make a larger piece of fabric? Whatever your reason, the point is that the love of making quilts is rooted in fabric and thread and creating a whole out of pieces.

When you start, what do you start with? Is it the fabric color? The print? Is it a block pattern, or what you want to do with the block now that you know how to put it together? What is it that drives you to finish, at least the top of a quilt? The answers are as numerous as the number of people making quilts, and that, as we know, is a whole bunch.

And what about art quilts—not so much why make art quilts, but what drives such quilts? "Why do I want to make this particular quilt?" precedes "How do I construct it?" Again, the answers are as numerous as the people making art quilts; it might be a technique, the fabric, an idea, a picture, a love of cows or watermelons, or any combination thereof.

Then, when the quilt top is sewn together, the question becomes, what now? How shall I quilt it? How shall I bind it? What kind of batting shall I use? What fabric shall I use for a backing? And then there is the question that often governs the answers to the others: What is it going to be used for?

This is where I get back to beads. Remember beads? I usually start from the bead end and not the quilt aspect when designing quilts. I enjoy sewing them onto fabric, as in bead embroidery. The New Century Dictionary defines the word *embroider* as "to decorate with needle work, to adorn or embellish." The problem was that the style of bead embroidery I had first learned called for the whole design to be carried by the beads, and I would wind up covering most or all of the fabric with beads. It was not mere embellishment. And it was time consuming in the extreme. Sewing beads on quilts gave me more texture than regular flat bead embroidery and allowed me to leave areas of fabric exposed. When I looked at quilts that had beads sewn onto them, I saw little dabs of beads here and there. One had to get up very close to even see the beads. My quest became to find the balance between the fabric and the beads and to give both a voice in the design, rather than to use

beads to embellish the design. Why? Because I liked beads, and I wanted a larger canvas to use them on. Having painted with watercolors and inks, with oils, and with acrylics, painting with beads was a logical step in making pictures, with fabric as the canvas.

Going back to choices for a moment, showcasing beads became my main reason for making small art quilts. Needle and thread, fabric and beads, handwork—all working together to make something that didn't exist before. You might want your piece to say something as simple as "I'm pretty," or something very important to you. In the beginning, most of my pieces were driven by what was printed on the fabric. Now, I might augment the printed design with Sharpie waterproof pens, dyes, or paint first, but mostly I use beads to draw lines, create texture, and add sparkle.

Back to the original question: "Why use beads?" My answer is "I love them! I love their infinite variety, size, shape, color, and finish, and what they can add to a surface." Why use plain stitching when you can use a bead with a color or finish that will add to the surface? Should you become a "beadaholic" like me, you may find yourself using beads for everything, when a piece of couched yarn or some machine top stitching would suffice. While we're asking questions, why not ask, "When do you stop?" Answer: "When you're done!" or, more precisely, "When you've reached the proper density of beads for that piece and have a balance between the beads and the fabric." Of course, there are other factors to be considered, such as when you've run out of time or patience … or you've run out of beads.

Early Frost, 2007, 9″ × 13″

Because They're There

Why incorporate beads into the designing of your quilt? Because beads are beautiful in and of themselves, and they do things that can't be done easily any other way. Sprinkle a few teardrops of clear glass with an AB (Aurora Borealis) finish over the surface of a leaf and you have raindrops. Run clear hex beads around a leaf and you have frost, or use lines of various sizes of clear Iris seed beads to create bubbles in a stream of water. Sometimes pieces, such as *Early Frost,* are designed around the beading because you want to work with an effect. At other times, a piece needs beads and you have to figure out what will work with that piece. There are times when I put beads on a quilt just because that's what I do. When the quilt top is finished, I go through my bead stash and see what will work and then go shopping for what I don't have but want to see on that quilt. The following section contains suggestions as to how you might start thinking in terms of where you could use beads to create a specific visual effect.

Designing Pieces around Wonderful Beads

Sometimes you have, are given, or buy beads that you just love but don't know what to do with. The green Chinese turquoise beads that form the snake in *Tenuous Membrane* are just such an example. I bought two strands of large, flat, irregularly shaped Chinese turquoise beads at a gem show because I liked them. They sat around for a couple of months, and I finally decided I had to use them in something. I got out fabric that the turquoise would complement and dove in. The result was *Tenuous Membrane*.

Tenuous Membrane, 2010, 29″ × 44″

Chinese turquoise beads in *Tenuous Membrane* (page 11)

The quilt that emerged was designed around two things: merging the narrow strip of Kaffe Fassett fabric (all I had) on the left with the batik on the right, and creating a home for the large green turquoise beads. I used reverse appliqué to integrate the two fabrics, adding more color as needed to heighten the illusion of leakage back and forth across the line. The head of the snake is a cabochon (a gemstone which has been rounded and polished as opposed to faceted) of Chinese turquoise held to the fabric with a bezel of beads (page 74). The rest of the large green pieces are actually beads with holes through them, so they could be sewn on one at a time. I was careful to secure them all the way through to the back of the quilt and to go through each bead several times.

Examples of stone slabs with holes drilled through

NOTE

Most stone beads are drilled with a sharp-pointed drill entering the bead at each end and meeting in the middle. When the holes do not exactly meet, there is a tiny sharp point in the hole that can cut any kind of thread. When using stone beads on fabric, be sure they lie flat and cannot move around, thereby causing friction and cutting the threads used to secure the beads. It would be wise to go through the hole as many times as the diameter allows.

Hole drilled in stone bead

Stone and shell discs with large holes can be sewn on with the same or a different color of thread, which can become a design element in itself.

Blue and white magnetite and various shell discs

Another example of a quilt designed around beads is *Partial Eclipse*. I wanted to work in BRIGHT colors! I got out some vintage bugle beads in a strange tomato color, some large vintage nailhead beads in a bright red-orange, some dyed turquoise discs of magnetite that I wanted to feature, and some pointy little oval nailheads in a yellow-orange. Then, getting out fabric in colors that sang to me, I pieced and reverse appliquéd a quilt top to put all those beautiful beads on. The piece was designed for the blue turquoise discs and the nailhead beads and as a venue for lots of bugle beads. Note also the purple and green background with dots; some are fabric, and some are beads. Halfway through beading the piece, I was reminded that availability is a design element. I discovered that I was about to run out of the bugle beads and pointy oval nailheads, so I faced the question of whether this design element would be sparse or lavish. I contacted the merchant I bought them from, and fortunately, more of both were available, so I could be lavish.

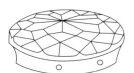

Nailhead beads have two sets of holes and are usually concave.

Round, orange, and pointy oval nailhead beads in *Partial Eclipse* (page 106)

Creating Texture

Partial Eclipse is also an example of creating texture with beads. Note the very different textures created with bugle beads. On the "sun" I used bugles in a random pattern, especially around the edges, to denote movement and instability. On the "moon" the bugles become part of the design of the pattern, running parallel to the lines in the fabric and also around the outside edges to give a soft-edge look and extend the color beyond the actual edge.

In the "land" at the bottom, I used the large vintage bugles with seed beads on top to suggest grass or at least something growing. By placing clumps of beads with the bottoms of the stalks closer than the tops, I was able to texture and quilt the area.

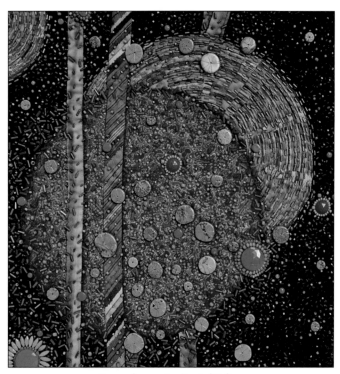

Sun and moon in *Partial Eclipse*

Grass in *Partial Eclipse* (page 106)

In *My Father's Shadow*, I did the same thing only more so. All the lines of bugles and seed beads extend upward and outward from a central area to suggest clumps of grasses. Note how perspective is achieved by creating shorter, smaller clumps as the grass recedes up the hill. I went from using two or three beads per grass blade to one bead, and then I finally had to resort to breaking the beads in half and sanding the sharp edges to do the final clumps.

Grass in *My Father's Shadow* (page 99)

Sky in *Australian Dreamscape* (page 104)

Single seed beads (page 51) and stacks (page 55) can also be used to add color or punch up color in an area. In the sky of *Australian Dreamscape*, I used beads and colored Sharpie pens to merge the three fabrics into one whole. All three fabrics have dots on them, and I recolored some of those dots with pens. Then, I filled some of the dots with seed beads, quilting the surface and suggesting that there are many more beads than there actually are. Notice the abalone button blanks with beaded bezels (page 74).

The sky of *Partial Eclipse* was created in a similar fashion. It is a dotted batik fabric, and I used #8 color-lined blue seed beads to deepen the color of the sky. Then, quilting through all the layers of fabric and batting, I added #11 turquoise, red, and orange beads to extend to the sky and carry color further from the larger beads. The blue, turquoise, and orange beads were all sewn on at the same time, as I was working area by area rather than color by color. Notice that the red and orange beads get smaller the farther they are from their "planets."

Sky in *Partial Eclipse* (page 106)

Beads as Lines

In *At Risk*, I wanted to incorporate lots of insects. My parents were both entomologists, and they enjoyed gardening. I wanted to create something that included both elements as a memorial to them and the garden that they had lavished some twenty-odd years of love and hard work on. I was working in the kaleidoscope venue (thank you, Paula Nadelstern) and decided I needed a spiderweb to catch some of the moths and butterflies I had gathered for the piece. Thinking of how stunning spiderwebs look all spangled with dew, I put the web in, line by line, with clear glass beads. The main support lines were plotted out first and drawn in with chalk. Then, the short lines went in, spiraling out from the center. Because the web had been built into the framework of the piece, it looked like it belonged there. The web had to have a spider, so I commissioned a friend to do a lampwork bead for the body. I gave him an enlarged photo of a yellow garden spider, and he gave me back the beautiful bead you see in the photos. I added long, shiny black bugle beads for legs, and the result was something only beads could have done.

Web and spider in *At Risk* (page 100)

Kaffe Fassett fabric without beads

Connections, 2010, 15½″ × 20″

Connections was a quilt I designed for a demonstration of mirror bezels. Using some of my favorite Kaffe Fassett fabric, I appliquéd the flowers and then machine stitched the lines around the petals and between the flowers. Next, I placed mirrors in the centers of the flowers, using beaded bezels (page 74). Then, I beaded over the stitched lines of the flowers and around each petal, carrying the silver of the mirrors and the beads around the mirrors into the flowers. I beaded the lines connecting the flowers with pale lavender #15 silver-lined beads, so they would be "almost there"; they connected the flowers more than the stitching did, but not as noticeably as if I had used the same beads as around the petals. This is an example of working with the lines in the fabric, as well as creating lines over the fabric.

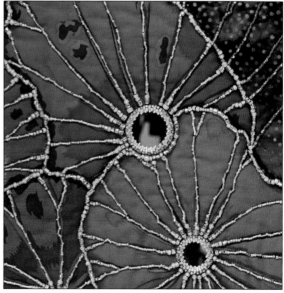

Flowers in *Connections*

August—thank you, Kaffe Fassett—is another example of beads as lines, using the same fabric but different beads. Note the change of color values in the piece as the lines in the flowers repeat existing colors in the fabric. The color of the center stones also gives depth to the piece that is quite different from the mirrors in *Connections*.

Beads, Tools, and Materials

There are whole books devoted to old beads, new beads, and beads made of glass, stone, polymer, bone, metal, and so on. My intent here is only to give you an idea of what shapes work well on quilts, leaving the finding of what you like to use up to you. Because this is a book about sewing beads onto quilts, we will look at the kinds of beads, the finishes, and the sizes and shapes available that work well with quilts. For now, let's look mainly at contemporary beads made of glass.

The Beads

Seed Beads

The base for most of my designing is the seed bead, so called because of its distinctive seedlike shape. Seed beads are made by heating a long, hollow tube of glass until it is almost molten, and then stretching the tube until it is the appropriate diameter. It is then chopped into the appropriate-sized pieces. The pieces are screened to take out the ones that are too big, and then they are put into a kiln and heated until they are almost, but not quite, molten. This rounds the edges and gives them the distinctive seed shape.

Graduated lines of seed beads, same color and graduated color

Seed beads come in many sizes, which are assigned numbers. Like needles and wire gauges, the larger the number, the smaller the size. I've been told that the number indicates the number of beads that equal an inch. These sizes are only an approximate indicator of how large the bead is. You will find variation within a particular batch of beads and from manufacturer to manufacturer. In general, Czech seed beads are more erratic in size and shape than Japanese beads.

The most common size used is #11; you will find these in the broadest array of colors and finishes, and they are most readily available. The tiniest beads I use are #14 and #15. When I was first starting to bead, I used to think that these were way too small for my large hands. I now use them a great deal. I always buy colors or finishes I like of the small beads when I see them, even if I may already have some, because they are not as readily available as #11 or #8. Seed beads go up in size to #6 and #4, and I often use a sequence of #6, #8, and #11,

and then finish off with #15, all of the same color, for a nice tapered line. Finding all those sizes in the same color is difficult, and sometimes I will use a lighter shade of a color for the smallest bead and graduate to darker, or vice versa, depending on the effect I want and the availability of the beads.

One more type of seed bead, which I do not use often, is the Japanese Delica. These beads are more tube shaped, rather than barrel shaped. Delicas are known for their regularity of size, in both length and diameter, and are wonderful for doing peyote stitch amulet bags or other off-loom bead weaving. I, however, find their regularity boring. Sometimes one wants beads all the same size and shape, but in general, I prefer the Czech beads with their charming irregularity.

With seed beads, you can make dots of color and lines, thick or thin. You can even fill in solid spaces with a particular color, which will give it texture.

Hex, Triangle, Cube, and Bugle Beads

Hex (or hexagonal), triangle, and cube refer to the shape of the cross section of the bead, and these beads also come in various sizes. Having flat sides that are at angles to the surface, they reflect tiny spots or short lines of light and can be used to add sparkle to a piece. They are more tube shaped, being longer than they are wide, and are usually a little longer than a seed bead of the same size designation. Use them for angularity and a little more visual weight.

Square beads of hematite and a large square bead of tigereye for focal points, with lines of cubes, bugle beads, hex, and triangle beads around them

Bugle beads are a longer tube of glass and may be round, hexagonal, or twisted. They will create lines of light that read across a room, especially the silver-lined beads. They are made basically the same way as seed beads, with a tube of glass stretched out to the appropriate diameter, both exterior and interior, and then chopped into segments of varying lengths, usually denoted in millimeters. Because of their nature, they are not usually put in a kiln after cutting, and the edges can be sharp. Thread passing over the lip of a bead at a right angle is vulnerable to being cut. How many garments have you seen with threads sticking out and beads missing? To prevent this, the bugle beads can be bracketed by putting a seed bead at each end. Some finishes will, by their nature, round the edges. To matte a bead, the beads are put into an acid bath, which etches the surface, thereby rounding the sharp edges. Metallic and AB (Aurora Borealis) finishes are fired on, and the heat rounds the edges as well. These beads need not be bracketed, but the rule of thumb is, "When in doubt, bracket."

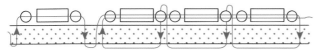

Bracketed single bead and bracketed couched beads

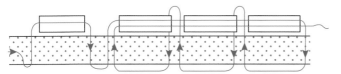

Single unbracketed bead and unbracketed couched beads

NOTE

■ Bugle beads go in and out of fashion, and vendors carry what they can sell of what is available. Specific colors or finishes of bugle beads sometimes become unavailable. As I write this, the available variety of Japanese bugle beads in matte and metallic finishes is diminishing. Manufacturers simply aren't making them at this time. Glittery, silver-lined, twisted bugle beads are available in many colors, but not many in metallic or matte.

■ Rule of thumb: Like yarns, the colors of beads can change, sometimes drastically, from lot to lot, so when you see a color, size, or finish you like, buy more than you think you will need. Or buy as many as you can afford; they may not be available next month, and availability is one of your design elements.

Pressed Glass Beads

Depending on the shape and size, pressed glass beads are made, either singly or in small lots, in a mold with molten glass. The colors and finishes available are almost as numerous as the shapes. Pressed glass beads, like seed beads, may be clear, translucent, or opaque. Color is infused by adding chemicals to the silica base. The amount and kind of chemicals added determine whether the glass is translucent or opaque. Then the bead may be sprayed with a metallic finish or something to give it a rainbow shimmer. The rainbow finishes can be either opaque (called AB for Aurora Borealis) or transparent (called Iris). The color of the bead itself may not be visible under the finish. The surface also may be matted by use of chemical etching, so the surface might be an AB matte finish on an opaque or translucent bead. Some of these finishes are baked on; some are just washes or dips. All are subject to wear, which in art quilts is not as important a factor as when the beads are used in jewelry or on clothing, but it is still something to be considered.

NOTE

When buying beads, it is advisable to know your vendors and ask them about the various finishes if you have any doubts. Some finishes are subject to fading in direct sunlight, and some are subject to wear. Again, with art quilts, the impact of sun and wear will be minimal but should be taken into consideration before buying the beads. Unless you know a vendor regularly stocks certain beads, my rule of thumb here is, "If you like the color and the size, and will probably use them, buy them! You may never see them again."

Some of the many shapes of pressed glass beads available include leaves, flowers, animals, fish, skulls, butterflies, and claws. Flat geometric shapes include circles, ovals, hexagons, donuts, lentils, triangles, squares, and cubes. The beads I find easiest to use are generally ones that have at least one flat side. How the hole goes through the bead is also important, and here the beads fall into three general categories: holes straight through lengthwise, vertical holes, and horizontal holes through one end of the bead.

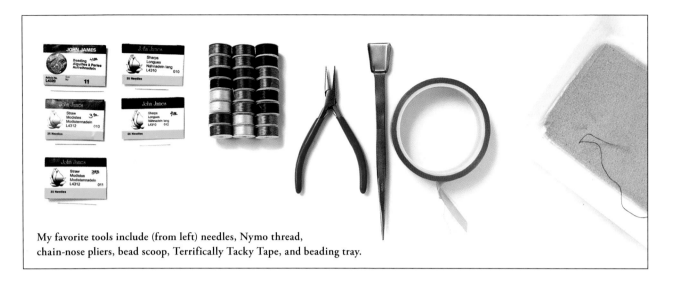

My favorite tools include (from left) needles, Nymo thread,
chain-nose pliers, bead scoop, Terrifically Tacky Tape, and beading tray.

Needles, Thread, Scissors, and Other Useful Tools

Needles

All the needles I refer to are a brand made in England called John James. I use three types and two or three diameters of each. The length of the needle is referred to by name: sharps, straws, or beading needles. The diameter of the needle is referred to in number form: #12, #11, or #10 (again, the larger the number, the smaller the diameter).

SHARPS

Sharps are the shortest of the three types I use, about an inch long. They are too short for my taste, but they do come in handy for maneuvering in tight spaces, and I am not as likely to turn one into a pretzel. The #11 is my preferred diameter when using sharps. When I need a needle that will pass through a very small hole, #12 is the one I use, and I use #10 only when all the beads I'm using have big enough holes.

STRAWS

Straws are my needle of choice and are currently only available in #11s and #10s. I'm told they are called such because the diameter is the same the entire length of the shaft, including the eye. The #11 straw is the needle I use most of the time. I have large hands and grip the needle firmly, so I am prone to turning needles into corkscrews. The #10 needles seem to be the most resistant to this, but they will not go through most #15 seed beads, some #11 seed beads, or almost any pearl. Hence, I usually use #11s and switch to #10s only when I can, like when I'm basting or am using only beads with large holes.

BEADING NEEDLES

I usually use beading needles only for fringe, since they are too long for most tight places and are cumbersome, even for couching (and I turn them into complicated corkscrews very quickly). They are available in sizes #12, #11, and #10. When I'm going to make a lot of fringe, my beading needle of choice is a #11, provided I am using a wide selection of beads with similar-sized holes.

NOTE

Pearls are notorious for having small holes! They come in a wonderful variety of colors, shapes, and sizes, but those tiny holes! When using Nymo thread (page 26) and a #12 needle of any type, you can pass through only once or twice. It is almost always necessary to use a #12 needle if you are going to use pearls or #15 or #14 seed beads in the strand. Remember that the number designation refers to the diameter, not the length.

Nymo Thread

My sister, Robin Atkins, a well-known bead artist, introduced me to Nymo thread, and it has become my thread of choice. Nymo is synthetic thread and is made up of many very thin fibers. Nymo comes in several weights, but B and D are the weights I use the most, because they are readily available and fit through most bead holes. This thread is very strong and comes in many colors, in bobbin or spool form. It also comes in cones of black or white.

I started by using bobbins but found I would go through four or five of them in a medium-size quilt. This meant I was sometimes changing color, especially when I had run out of one color before finishing the quilt. Changing the color of the thread is occasionally, but not often, desirable, at least for me. I now try to keep a number of spools in stock in colors I frequently use, so I can choose the thread color that will best blend with the back of my quilt.

I even use this thread for almost all of my hand sewing. It's much stronger than cotton or cotton/polyester, although it does sometimes tend to fray.

Scissors

Small scissors with sharp points and thin blades seem to work best for working with beads on quilts. The scissors I use most are Ginghers embroidery scissors. They fit my hand nicely, and I can get into small spaces to cut thread easily. Find the pair that works best for you. Test-drive them to be sure they cut thread well because sometimes you will be cutting very close to the beads.

Chain-Nose Pliers

Chain-nose pliers are not absolutely essential, but they do come in handy, and I resort to them frequently. When too many beads are on a piece of thread not long enough for them to sit side by side, one option is to take out the stitches. A much easier way to rectify the situation is to crush one or more of the beads. Chain-nose pliers are exactly the right size and shape to do that. The caveat here is that there is always the possibility of breaking the thread, and that possibility increases exponentially with the size of the bead. I've crushed a great many #11 seed beads and not broken the thread. However, when crunching #8 beads, the likelihood of breaking the thread greatly increases; #8s are also much more difficult to crush, requiring more strength. Always wear protective lenses and/or keep one hand over the bead to be crushed. Tiny pieces of glass do fly. The table and floor where I work are frequently littered with bits of broken beads.

Nymo thread bobbins

Chain-nose pliers

Batting

When I first started quilting and was faced with batting choices, cotton seemed to work best. Polyester required too much subduing and seemed too commercial. Bamboo batting seemed too exotic for me. Then, a fellow teacher told me that she always used Hobbs Wool. It is resin bonded to resist bearding and has a very nice loft, yet compresses easily for texture. I tried some, and now Hobbs Wool is my batting of choice if I want a lot of texture, for either hand sewing or machine quilting.

Backing

When choosing a backing for a quilt, I prefer to use a fabric with colors that relate to and support the face design. I used to only hand quilt, mainly with the application of the beads, and not use any machine sewing because I didn't like the combination of stitches on the back. One time, I was in a hurry and needed a piece for a demo that was mostly finished, so I machine quilted a great deal of it. I finished it with the beading and found that the combination of stitches on the back wasn't bad. Now I choose fabrics for the back with overall patterns that are small and busy, so the machine and hand stitches will not show too much. Batiks are always a good choice because the color varies within a small range and the fabric is a tight weave and gives the quilt lots of support.

I use a thread color that blends in with the color of the back for both machine and hand stitching. That way the stitches disappear, and you don't have to be quite as careful about stitch length. However, when a stitch is too long, as sometimes happens when you think you are traveling in the batting and have gone through to the back, use a waterproof Sharpie pen to camouflage the line. After all, even though no one is supposed to, everyone looks at the back! It might as well be pretty, too!

Terrifically Tacky Tape

Yes, that is really its name. I didn't make it up. Terrifically Tacky Tape is a double-sided transparent membrane that comes in rolls of varying widths and is generally available at craft stores. It is usually used for scrapbooking; I use it to secure cabochons, buttons, or certain beads, when I want to hold them in place to sew them down or create bezels. It comes with iodine-colored plastic film covering one side. Make sure the tape is at least 1″ wide. I buy rolls that are 5′ long, and they seem to last forever. You should avoid using your good scissors when cutting tacky tape because they will get gummy. Although that is not a disaster, because the goo is fairly easy to clean off, it still is a bother.

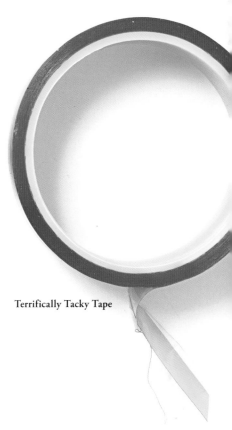

Terrifically Tacky Tape

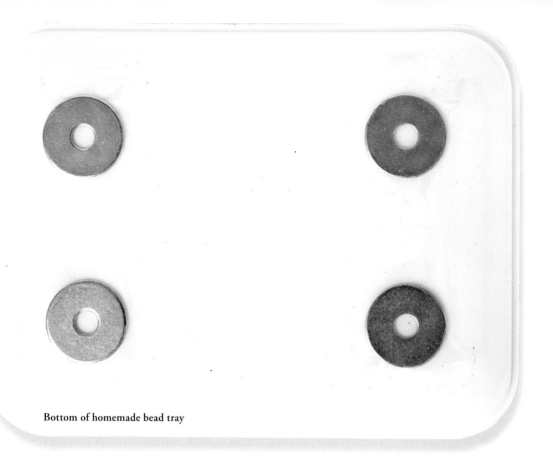

Bottom of homemade bead tray

Bead Cloths and Trays

A bead cloth is useful for putting out a large assortment of beads on a flat surface where you can easily pick them up with a needle. I like to use the commercially available bead cloths made out of something such as Polartec or a similarly thin synthetic fleece. The fleece comes in a variety of colors, but I prefer a neutral off-white or pale gray-green. It depends, of course, on the color of the beads you are using. Small off-white beads are difficult to see on an off-white cloth. Bead cloths should be small enough so you can turn them around to reach all the beads.

I've come to like the portability of small bead trays when working on large artworks. I make them out of shallow white Styrofoam meat trays that I line with Polartec cut to size and secured with Terrifically Tacky Tape or adhesive tape. Because the trays are very light—and a flick of the finger can scatter beads widely—I tape four large metal washers to the underside with packing tape to help stabilize them. I make them in several sizes, so I can put them right on the quilt where I'm working and move them around at will. I will frequently work with two or three different trays with different assortments of colors and sizes of beads in each.

Bead Scoops

I have made my own bead scoop from one of my grandmother's silver teaspoons by cutting the end off, flattening out the bowl, and then filing a beveled edge, so I can gather up beads when I am through with them and return them to the plastic bags in which I store them. There is a commercially available version that is a combination of scoop and tweezers. The corners of the scoop can be used to corral runaway beads back into neat piles and to sort out strays.

Bead scoop

Basic Stitches

There are four basic stitches for bead embroidery: single (or seed) stitch, lazy stitch, back stitch, and couching. There are also edging stitches, fringes, and lots of variations. I use single stitch for dots of color, a combination of couching and back stitch for lines, and lazy stitch only when I want solid areas of beading. The picot edge stitches and fringes are used to add texture and elevation to a piece. As you work with the stitches and learn what they do, you will find your favorites.

Preparing to Bead

Stretching the Thread

Always stretch your thread before using it. Nymo has a little give, and it is better to release it before starting to bead. If you do not stretch the thread before using it, the weight of the beads will do it for you over time, and the thread will loosen on the surface of your quilt.

Photo by Carole Trengove

Stretching thread

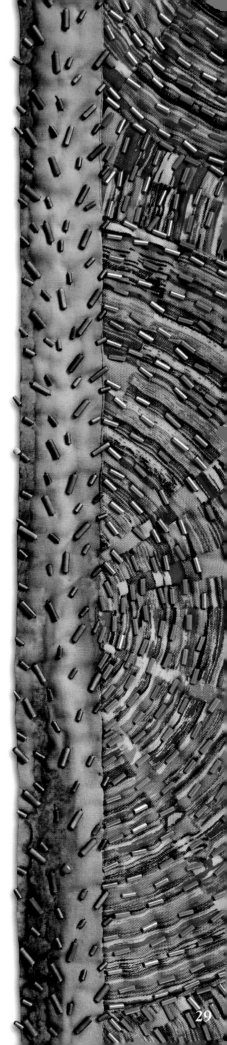

Threading Needles

Many people have trouble threading needles and, as a consequence, use a very long thread, which can be cumbersome and result in tangling and knotting. This is annoying in the extreme and to be avoided at all costs. You can do several things to facilitate threading. First, always use a freshly cut end to thread through the eye. Cut it cleanly at an angle. Then, after wetting the end, pull it through your thumb and forefinger to give it a chisel shape. Rotate the thread until the sharp edge of the chisel is parallel to the needle's eye. Hold the needle in your dominant hand, and with the thread held in your other hand, about ½″ in from the end, thread the needle. It helps to hold the eye of the needle and the end of the thread over a plain white surface. You can see both the hole and the end of the thread more clearly. I use the back of a business card or the edge of my bead tray.

Knotting the Thread

You will be knotting thread frequently. If you are pulling the knot through the fabric face to bury it, you will want to control the size of the knot. The knot I use is one my sister, Robin, taught me. It is similar to a French knot; some know it as a quilter's knot. It can be difficult and confusing initially, especially if you are using the wrong portion of the thread or wrapping it in the wrong direction, but once you've got it, you'll really like it.

1. Hold the threaded needle in your dominant hand between your thumb and forefinger. Lay the thread end, the end farthest from the needle, across the needle. Where you lay the thread is where the knot will end up.

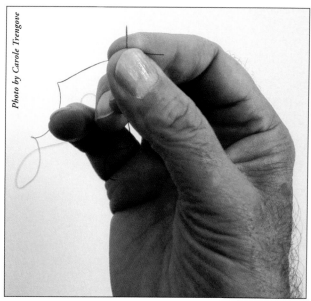

Photo by Carole Trengove

Holding threaded needle in dominant hand, lay thread end, end farthest from needle, over needle.

2. Continuing around the needle in the direction of travel, wrap the thread 4 to 5 times around the needle. The number of wraps needed will vary a little depending on the tightness of the weave of the fabric you are pulling the knot through. (This is for a single thread; if using a double thread, wrap 2 or 3 times.)

With your other hand, take hold of the needle tip and, holding tight to the wrapped thread with your thumbnail, pull the needle through your thumb and forefinger and keep sliding the wrap down to the end of the thread. If you lose hold of the wrap, start over.

Remember, where you lay the thread across the needle is where the knot will end up, so if you want a short tail, lay only a short length of thread across the needle. This will always give you a knot of a specific size, and by being careful where you lay the thread over the needle, you won't have to pick up a pair of scissors and trim the tail before starting. No more spitting on your fingers and winding up with an ill-defined wadded mess somewhere close to the end of the thread.

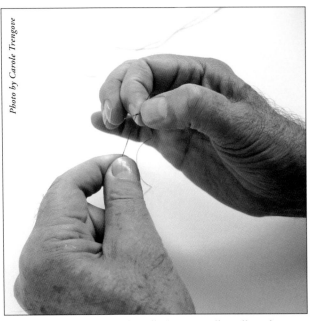

Wrap thread around needle 4 times; pull needle and following thread through to end.

Burying the Knot

When pulling the knot through the material, the size of the knot is governed by the type of material you are going through. Batiks are printed with dye that penetrates all the way through, and the weave is very tight. A four-wrap knot works best for this. For prints of a looser weave, where the dye or paint sits on the surface, a five-wrap knot would be preferable. When you pull to bury the knot, you may get what looks like a run in the material. In this case, start the threads on the back or leave the knot on the surface and come up from the batting where you wish to start sewing on beads. Tie a pair of overhand knots (see page 32) to anchor the thread, and then trim off the knot.

In pulling the knot through, insert the needle in the cloth face and go through to the batting. Travel in the batting a greater distance than the length of the tail to the spot where you wish to place the first bead. Come up to the surface and gently but firmly pull the thread until the knot "pops" through the surface fabric and into the batting. I like to dip the needle down for a tiny stitch on the back before coming up to the surface. This way the first bead is anchored through to the back. Be careful not to pull the knot all the way through to the back. If you come back later and trim it off, the beads will begin to fall off the surface.

Tying Knots on the Surface

When sewing on larger beads, I like to use a double thread, or if using a single thread, I pass through at least three times. I also do a lot of knot tying on the surface of the piece rather than turn it over and knot on the back.

SINGLE OVERHAND KNOT

1. To tie a single overhand knot, bring your needle through the batting and up to the surface of the quilt. Leaving a little slack on the surface, go through all the layers of the quilt sandwich to the back. Come back up to the surface in approximately the same spot where you started and loop through the slack. Pull the thread tight to form a knot on the surface.

2. Put the needle back into the batting and travel to the spot where you want to place your first bead.

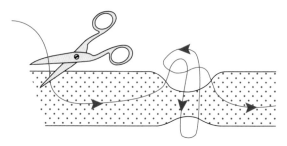

DOUBLE OVERHAND KNOT

1. Begin by following Step 1 of the Single Overhand Knot (above).

2. Again, leave a little slack on the surface and bring the needle all the way to the back of the quilt. Bring the needle back to the front of the quilt and loop through the slack.

3. Pull the thread tight to form a double knot on the surface. Put the needle back into the batting and travel to the spot where you want to place your first bead.

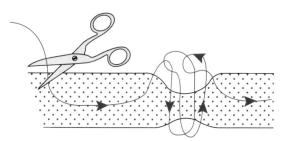

Four Basic Stitches

I have adapted these stitches from regular bead embroidery, where the artist works on a single thickness of fabric and usually wants the beads to lie flat on a flat surface. When working on a quilt, you can embed the beads in the surface and use their application to do a great deal of the quilting. It is a little more work than regular embroidery (where it's acceptable for the back to be a mess) because in quilting, the look of the back is important. Consequently, you will want to travel in the batting and knot frequently. From here on I will discuss three general categories of beads: seed beads, usually referred to by number (page 20); bugle beads, usually designated by length (in millimeters); and large or novelty beads, usually referred to by size (in millimeters) or shape (such as triangle, teardrop, hex, leaf, flower shape, and so on).

NOTE

Use single thread except when otherwise indicated.

Single Stitch or Seed Stitch

Sometimes called seed stitch, single stitch is one of the simplest stitches and can be very useful to create texture, dotted lines, and short stacks, and to secure large flat beads.

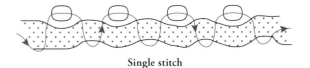

Single stitch

1. Starting with a single thread, bury the knot and come up from the back of the fabric to where you want to place the first bead.

2. Pick up a single seed bead on your needle, go back down through the quilt right next to the bead, and then come up where you want the next bead. Continue to sew on beads.

If the bead is lying tipped at an angle, with the hole to the sky, you probably inserted the needle into the fabric too close to where you came up, thereby not giving the bead enough thread to sit on. If the thread shows, you most likely inserted the needle too far away from the bead. Of the two, it's better to have too much thread showing than not enough thread for the bead to sit on.

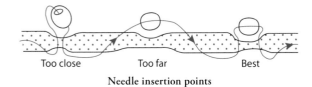

Too close   Too far   Best

Needle insertion points

You can cover an area with dots, quilting as you go, or make dotted lines with just the single stitch technique.

If you want more space between the beads than ¼″, you can achieve a smaller stitch on the back if your needle enters the fabric sandwich at an angle and goes back up at an angle to the top.

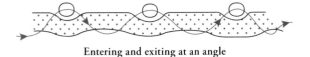

Entering and exiting at an angle

You also can vary the number of beads in each segment, using up to 4 beads, and/or vary the size of the bead and the kind of bead.

Varying number, size, and shape of beads

If you want a plain dotted line, use a running stitch with a bead on the surface of each stitch, sewing all the stitches through to the back. By carefully aligning all the bead holes along the same axis, a dotted line will appear to be one continuous line.

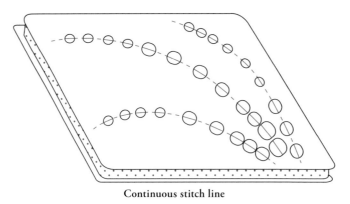

Continuous stitch line

If you are texturing a large area, knot through all the fabrics when you start and finish the area or when you run out of thread. A pair of simple overhand knots (page 32) usually is sufficient. How frequently you knot is entirely your choice. The more security you need, the more frequently you knot in between beads.

STACKS

Stacks are a variation of the single stitch.

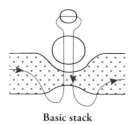

Basic stack

1. Starting with a single thread, come up from the back of the fabric to where you want the first bead.

2. Pick up 2 or more beads on your needle and pull them down the thread to the fabric. The last, or topmost, bead will hereafter be referred to as the "anchor bead."

3. Bypassing the anchor bead, go back down through the rest of the beads and through to the back. If it is a tall stack, pull tight, holding the anchor bead, and knot on the back before going on to the next stack.

If you want to change the position of the stack just slightly, you can do so by coming back up through the whole stack, going through the anchor bead, and going back down to the fabric; move the needle over to reposition the stack before reentering the fabric. Making stacks is a good way to sew on sequins, heishi, or roundels. I frequently use a #15 seed bead for the anchor bead if I do not wish to cover too much of the bead underneath.

Stack Variations

The variations are endless, depending on the availability of beads, your imagination, and what you wish to achieve. Stacks can create a raised area or texture above the surface of the quilt. The possibilities include using many beads, varying the beads in the stack, starting with a large bead and going progressively smaller to achieve a tapered look, or using more than one bead for an anchor bead.

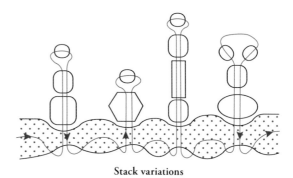

Stack variations

LOOPS

Loops are stacks that have been tipped over on their side and secured to the surface at each end.

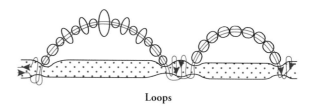

Loops

1. Starting with a single thread, bury the knot and come up from the back of the fabric to where you want the first bead.

2. Pick up the desired number of beads with the needle, slide them up snug to the fabric, and enter the fabric closer to the exit point than the length of the beads on the thread. Go through all the layers.

Where you re-enter the fabric determines how high above the surface the loop will be. You would be well advised to go back through the loops to reinforce them, because they are vulnerable to being snagged. You could even pass through a third time and thus be in position to continue in the direction of travel. It is a good idea to knot before and after each loop.

Back Stitch

Use this stitch for making short, continuous lines of beads, straight or curved, either restating lines already in the fabric's design or creating new ones.

1. Starting with a single thread, come up from the back of the fabric to where you want the first bead.

2. String 5 to 7 beads on your thread, depending on the size of the beads (5 #8 beads and up to 7 #11 beads).

3. Holding the thread taut, push the beads back to where you came up through the fabric and then push the needle down through to the back, just past the last bead (not too close to or too far from the starting point).

Needle inserted too close to starting point

Needle inserted too far from starting point

4. Depending on the number of beads used in each section, come back up close to the center of the section between beads and go through the last 3 or 4 beads again.

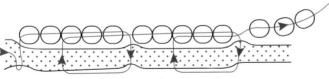

Back stitch

5. Repeat Steps 1–4 as many times as necessary to extend the line as far as you wish to go.

If you are going around tight curves, try using only 4 beads at a time, back stitching every 2 beads. This helps secure the beads to the fabric and keeps the curves even.

6. Knot through all the layers at the end of the line.

You can go back through all the beads in the line one or more times, thereby reinforcing the line and smoothing out the waggles. This stitch is best used for short solid lines such as branches going out from a leaf or flower stem. I like to taper lines when I can, working from #8 beads to #11 to #15. This gives a lovely organic look.

If the beads move back and forth on the thread, push all the beads back to the previous stitch, snugly without crowding, and then go straight down to the back and do a back stitch. As you exit the last bead in the line, start the next segment immediately. This covers the excess thread from the previous segment and keeps the line continuous.

> **NOTE**
>
> If the beads don't lie well on the fabric but push each other out of line, you need to give the beads a little more thread. I sometimes call these unwanted loops "croquet hoops." Think of them as a row of people trying to stand shoulder to shoulder on a plank that is not long enough to accommodate all the people in a straight line. To get a straight line, you have to push some of the people off the plank. So crush unwanted beads (see Chain-Nose Pliers, page 26).

Couching

In sewing, little stitches are used to secure or "couch" a straight or curved line of thread, yarn, or ribbon onto the fabric. This works just as well with beads.

1. Starting with a single thread, bury the knot, take a tiny stitch through to the back, and come up where you want the first bead. Thread a line of as many as 15 or more beads onto your needle.

Bead size being variable, I think in terms of needle lengths rather than numbers of beads. When I'm couching, my needle of choice is a #11 John James straw (page 25). I sometimes work with 1½ needles' worth of beads at a time—that is 1½"–2" of beads. They may be of different or the same sizes, shapes, and colors.

2. Slide the beads down to the fabric, pulling the thread taut. Push the needle straight down through all the layers of fabric, a little past the end of the beads.

3. Come up 3 or 4 beads back and a little to one side. Cross over the thread and go back down on the other side of the thread through all the layers.

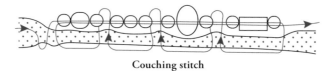

Couching stitch

4. Working your way back, repeat Step 3 the entire length of the line.

If you are going to continue the line, go forward through all the beads again and proceed with the next segment of beads. It is a good idea, when working a straight line, to come up each time on the same side of the thread holding the line of beads.

When going around a curve, come up on the inside of the curve and pull the line out to the place you want it. You can use the thumb on your nondominant hand to push the line of beads to where you want it, and then bring the needle up on the inside of the curve for the next loop over the thread. Work your way around the curve, tacking the beads in place as you go. Doing a curve this way is much easier than trying to come up exactly in the right place on the outside of the curve and then going back down on the inside.

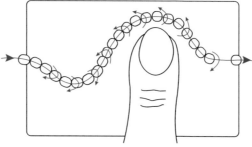

Push strand in place with thumb

■ Keep the couching stitches perpendicular to the thread carrying the beads and come up between beads and not in the middle of a bead. It is a good idea to allow a little extra thread at the end of each couched segment before going down to the back. You will most likely use it up by the time you get back to the beginning of the segment, and the tendency is to bunch the beads toward either end of the segment.

■ If you are doing a long curve or a series of short curves, lay the line of beads across the curves as far as the beads will go and start couching back from that point. This will provide you with enough space for all the beads without crowding as you go around the curves.

■ When couching, it is a good idea to pass back through the whole line of beads—all the segments— at least one time and sometimes more, to even out the kinks and bumps in the line. This is especially true with #8 beads because they tend to have larger holes, and the top and bottom of the bead may not be precisely parallel, causing the beads to go off at angles rather than staying in a straight line. Picture a line of unruly first graders and you have a typical line made from #8 seed beads.

■ Crush extraneous beads that do not have a place in the segment. Terrifying idea? When there are too many beads trying to occupy the same space, causing waggles in the line, try crushing (see Chain-Nose Pliers, page 26) the extraneous ones as a last resort. Be brave! Always have a needle and thread ready to go back through the line of beads in case you happen to break a main support thread so that you can salvage what you've done.

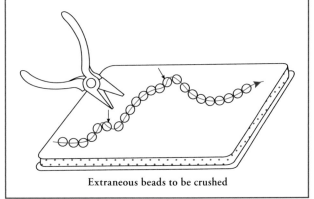

Extraneous beads to be crushed

Lazy Stitch

Lazy stitch is a convenient way to fill space with beads. American Indian beadwork uses this stitch to cover large areas with beads, filling in leaves, flowers, and background after the outlines have been established with back stitch or couching. Similar to a satin stitch in embroidery, you can use the lazy stitch to fill in areas, to make lines of varying width, or even to create texture.

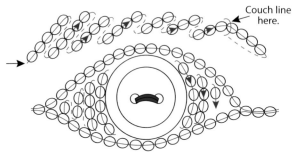

Lazy stitch, short parallel lines

1. Starting with a single thread, bury the knot and come up from the back of the fabric to where you want the first bead.

2. String up to 5 beads and, holding the thread taut with your thumb, push the beads back to where the thread came up through the fabric. Go down to the back and come up a bead's width from the point where you started at the beginning of the previous line.

3. Depending on the shape of the area you are filling, continue to lay down parallel lines of beads, either increasing or decreasing the number of beads in each line.

It is advisable to not exceed 5 beads (if you are using #11) in a line without some support. If you do exceed 5 beads, either couch or back stitch. You won't disturb the continuity of the line, and the beads won't be vulnerable to being snagged or caught. Because these longer segments would otherwise have a corresponding longer length of thread on the back, the slight diagonal of the shorter lines of thread is a good trade-off for one long line. Again, because vulnerability is a concern, as well as how it looks on the back, this is another excellent reason to keep the lines shorter, or broken by couching or back stitch.

The following variations of the lazy stitch can create different decorative effects.

BASKET STITCH

Because the eye perceives the alignment of the holes in a bead, you can create the illusion of a basket weave by making a series of squares formed of lines. By running the lines first vertically and then horizontally, you can give the impression of the beads weaving over and under each other.

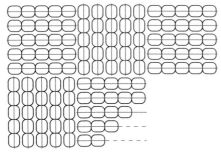

Basket stitch

1. Starting with a single thread, bury the knot and come up from the back of the fabric to where you want the first bead.

2. Start by stitching a square of 5 rows of 5 #11 seed beads parallel to one another using the lazy stitch (page 38).

3. Continue the line, but rotate the direction 90° for the next square, and so on.

To add depth to this illusion, you could use slightly darker beads at the ends of the rows where a square appears to go under the previous square.

HERRINGBONE

Whole borders can be made using the herringbone stitch (short, parallel angled rows of beads.)

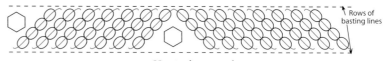

Rows of basting lines

Herringbone stitch

1. Starting with a single thread, bury the knot and come up from the back of the fabric to where you want the first bead.

2. Lay down the first row of beads, and then go down through the fabric to the back and bring the needle up next to the first bead in the first row. The row may be at an angle or perpendicular to the direction of travel, and the length of the row should not exceed the length of 5 #11 seed beads or it will be vulnerable to being snagged.

3. Lay the second row down next to and parallel to the first row, and continue to lay down parallel rows of beads until the desired band of beads is achieved.

4. If you include bugle beads, remember to check to see if the edges are sharp, and if so, bracket them with seed beads (page 23).

5. Changing directions makes an interesting variation. You can fill in the triangle with a single bead or a series of beads. You will find that one angle is easier to stitch than the other.

If you are not using a line or border printed on the fabric, it is easier to keep the lines straight if you draw chalk lines or baste a line of thread to delineate where the edges of the border are.

WANDERING PATH

The wandering path stitch can be used many ways, depending on what you wish to accomplish. It can be variable in width and content or used with all the same size and color of bead. It's dealer's choice—dependent only on your imagination and what beads you have available.

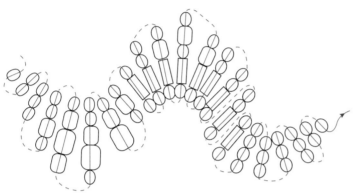

Wandering path

This stitch is accomplished the same way as the herringbone (page 39), except that the lines are not parallel, and you make it up as you go along. The same caveat applies about the length of the lines of beads. If a line is longer than 5 #11 seed beads or the equivalent, it needs to be couched (page 37) or back stitched (page 36). If you are changing the direction of the line instead of traversing the width of the row of beads on the underside of the fabric to start the next line, just move on the back of the quilt the appropriate distance, and come up to start the next line.

NOTE

Beads not secured through to the back will not produce texture but instead will lie flat on the surface of the piece. To produce this effect, travel in the batting rather than taking the stitch through to the back. I do this when I do not want the dimple or shadow found under the bead when tied through to the back, as in spots on the petal of a flower or in an area where I do not wish to have quilting but do want beads.

Fringes

We will deal with the use of fringe in more detail in Chapter 4, but suffice it to say that fringes are just long stacks (page 35). They can be attached anywhere and need not be on the edge of a piece.

I usually use a single thread for fringe because a double thread tends to make the strand stiff and inflexible. Working with a single thread is especially important when using pearls in the strand because pearls are notorious for having small holes, and you usually can't pass through them more than twice, even using a #12 needle.

1. Starting with a single thread, tie a knot and come up from the back of the fabric to where you want the first bead.

2. String the number of beads to the desired strand length. Bypassing the end bead (anchor bead, which can be more than one bead), come back through all the beads.

3. After returning to the fabric through the strand, hold the anchor bead and pull the thread tight. This eliminates the ¼″ or so of excess thread that is sometimes found between the beads and the body of the work. Knot at the fabric and go on to the next strand of fringe.

4. It is important to tie a knot after every strand of fringe. This way, if the thread breaks, or if you do not like that strand and decide to remove it, the strands on either side won't fall off as well. Beads on the floor are only a good thing as far as the cat is concerned, (and my wife likes the ping, ping they make in the vacuum cleaner).

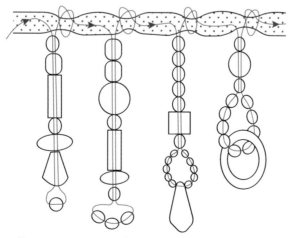

Fringe variations: Note how on some strands many beads are used as an anchor bead unit.

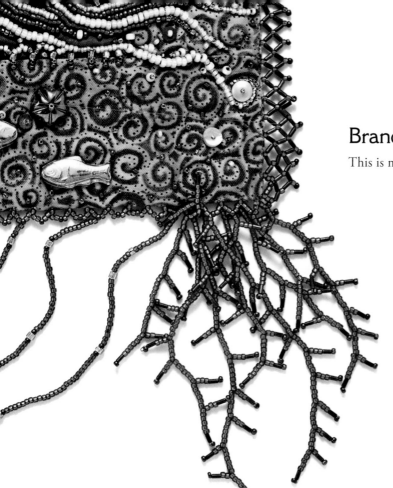

Branching or Coral Fringe

This is my favorite fringe and the one I use most often.

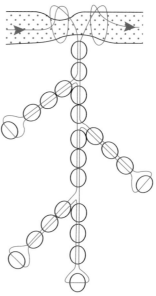

Branching or coral fringe

1. Starting with a single thread, tie a knot, and come up from the back of the fabric to where you want the first bead.

2. Collect beads on the needle until you have the length of strand you want. The last bead (or beads) on the strand is the anchor bead. Bypassing the anchor bead, return through the beads of the main strand to where you want the first branch.

3. Exit the main strand, add the beads for the branch, and, bypassing the anchor bead, return to the main stem.

4. Work your way up the main stem, exiting only where you want another branch, until you get back to the fabric.

Be careful to pull each branch tight to the main stem. If there is excess thread at the top of the main strand, start at the anchor bead at the end of the main strand and work the excess thread all the way up to the top through each branch in order.

Kinky Fringe

(Also Known as Zigzag Fringe)

This is the fringe you make inadvertently when you bypass a bead on the way up from the anchor bead in a single strand of fringe. I rarely use it as a design element, but when kinks happen, it's nice to know the reason for them and how to do it intentionally if you so desire.

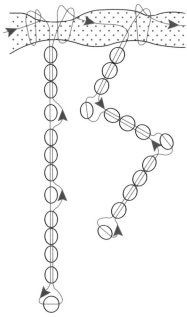

Kinky or zigzag fringe

1. Starting with a single thread, tie a knot and come up from the back of the fabric to where you want the first bead.

2. String a strand of beads to the desired length.

3. Return up the strand, bypassing the anchor bead, and bypass a bead to make a kink at each place in the strand where you desire a kink to happen. The strand must be pulled tight for it to kink. The tighter the thread is pulled, the more acute the angle of the kink. Knot while the thread is pulled to the desired degree of tightness for the kink to remain.

For a vivid demonstration, use a different color of bead where you want kinks in the strand and then bypass those beads on the way back up from the anchor bead at the end of the strand. The different-colored bead should be the "elbow" at each kink.

Single Picot Edge Stitch
(Sometimes Called a Single Bead Edge Stitch)

A picot edge is a beautiful way to finish the edge of a small piece, covering the join between the back and the front in lieu of a binding. It also can be used to join two sides of a piece that are right sides out. The thread will show with this variation, so use a color you wish to see against the beads, especially as this stitch requires a double thread.

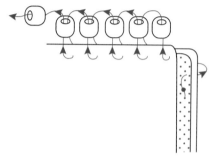

Single picot or single bead edge

1. Starting with a double thread, bury the knot and come up from the back of the fabric to where you want the first bead, preferably at a corner.

NOTE ———————————————
For right-handed people, start at a right-hand corner and work to the left. Left-handed people need to reverse the directions and work left to right.

2. Go through to the front, anchoring the thread.

3. Pick up 2 beads and take a shallow stitch (just deep enough to hold the bead in place) through the edge, from back to front.

4. With the needle, go back up through the second bead. This locks the second bead in place.

5. Move over the width of 1 bead from the center of the last bead, pick up another bead, and take another shallow stitch from back to front. Come back up through the bead just added and repeat.

6. When you have gone all the way around a piece, come back up through the first bead and continue to stitch through 2 or more beads to lock the first bead in place and secure the thread.

There are several things to watch for when first starting. They all have to do with spacing.

■ If the edge begins to look swaybacked, with the ends pulling in toward the center, the beads are too far apart and are being pulled together at the top.

■ If the edge begins to look like a ruffle, the beads are too close together and are jostling each other for space on the edge. You must allow a bead width from the center of the last bead. Crushing beads (Chain-Nose Pliers, page 26) will not serve you well here.

■ If the edge tilts toward the face or toward the back, you aren't taking your stitches straight through, from back to front. If you take a smaller amount of the back edge and more of the front, it will pull the beads to the front. By the same token, if you take more of the back edge than the front, it will pull the row of beads to the back. It is important to keep the depth of the stitch consistent, especially if the thread color shows up against the fabric. This is where those of you who stitch beautifully and evenly will shine. My borders are frequently a bit untidy, but that is consistent with the organic, handmade quality of my pieces and the irregularity of the beads.

■ Do not worry if it feels awkward at first. There is such a thing as muscle memory. You will develop a rhythm after you have completed a few inches, and your fingers will know what to do, leaving your mind free to wander or design further.

Variations on Single Picot

When I was just beginning to teach bead embroidery, a student came up to me in a class, complaining that she had done the single picot "all wrong" and that it "looked awful." She showed me a row of beads lying parallel to the edge instead of perpendicular. I told her that it wasn't what I had taught, and asked her to please show me what she had done as I liked the new variation she had just invented. She proceeded to do so and here is a single picot variation.

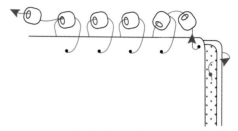

Single picot variation

1. Start with a buried knot on the right-hand corner and pick up 2 beads.

2. Pass down through the top of the second bead and pick up a bead. The direction you pass through the second bead is the only thing you change, but this pulls the bead parallel to the edge.

3. Continue by taking the next stitch a bead width from the center of the last bead. Go through, from back to front, and go down through the bead you just picked up.

NOTE

If you do not like the fact that the beads are parallel to each other but at an angle to the edge, you can pass through all the beads in that section of the edge at least one more time to reinforce and realign them.

Double Picot Edge Stitch

This stitch makes a nice lacy edge, looking somewhat like the crocheted edge used on pillowcases or doilies. It is important, however, to use beads that are all of the same width and thickness.

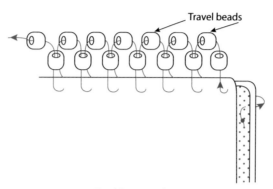

Double picot edge

1. Double picot is similar to single picot (page 44), except you start by picking up 3 beads instead of 2. Come back up through the last bead of the 3 and add 2 more beads.

2. Take a stitch a bead width away, from back to front, and come up through the second bead of the new pair, and so on. The second bead of the first 3, and thereafter the first bead of the new pair, is the travel bead.

It is important to be careful of the spacing. Too far apart and the travel bead will fall between the 2 beads perpendicular to the edge. Too close together and you will start to get a ruffle. It is also important to use beads that are consistent in both length and diameter. I once tore out several inches of a double picot border I had done with vintage faceted jet beads. They were beautiful beads of different sizes, and although they were right for the piece, their irregularity made the edge look sloppy.

Many variations on this stitch are possible when you change bead size, shape, or color. You also can add more travel beads between the base beads and create a multitude of variations. When you start to widen the space between the base beads of the picot, the spacing becomes crucial. Irregularities will call attention to themselves, and if you are doing more than one row, the irregularities will compound. Tiger Tape, which has regular intervals marked with black hash marks, is useful here to keep the spacing even. The following illustration shows one of my favorite variations.

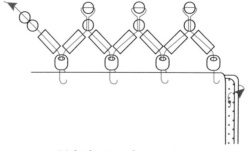

Multiple picot edge variation

Sewing Beads with Various Hole Placements

As you become more adventuresome in your bead buying, you will encounter beads that need special treatment in order to make them stay in place. Some are easier to sew on than others, but you may find that the bead you want for that particular place is one of the tough ones. Here are some ways of dealing with the vagaries of holes in beads.

Beads with Straight, Lengthwise Holes

Beads with straight, lengthwise holes are the easiest to make stay where you put them because they are secured on each side. Sometimes, when you're lucky, you'll find a bead with two parallel holes.

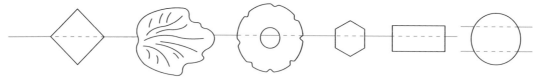

Single and double straight, lengthwise holes

1. To add beads with 2 parallel holes, bring the needle up at A and pass through 1 hole (A to B). Go down to the back and over to come up by the next hole on the same side of the bead (B to C).

2. Go back through the bead (C to D) and through to the back at D.

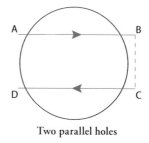

Two parallel holes

3. Repeat Steps 1 and 2, and then knot to secure the bead in place.

Beads with Vertical Holes

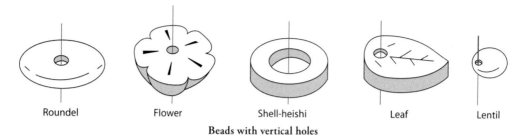

Roundel   Flower   Shell-heishi   Leaf   Lentil

Beads with vertical holes

Beads with holes vertically through them are easy, too. They include roundels, flowers, leaves, sequins, heishi (both seashell and eggshell), bone, stone, buttons, and so on. I frequently use them as bases for stacks, but there are several other treatments depending on the shape of the bead and how you want to use it.

For the leaf shape with a vertical hole in one end, you can use what I call a chicken foot stitch, taking three stitches. The first stitch (A) secures the bead to the cloth. The second (B), to one side of the first, helps stabilize the location and perhaps slightly change the position of the leaf. The third stitch (C) finishes locking the leaf so it will rotate only 60° or so.

For round beads with multiple rows of small seed beads down the sides, start with a basic stack (page 35). Come back up to one side of the hole through the large bead and figure out how many beads it will take to get from the cloth to the anchor bead. Put that many beads on the thread, pass through the anchor bead, and continue down the other side to the base. Come up to one side of that row and repeat as many times as desired, locking each row in place by a pass through the anchor bead. Handsome flower centers can be made this way.

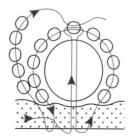

Sometimes you may have a bead with a vertical hole and want a number of stacks emerging from the center. Start with the first stack, return to the back of the piece, and come up again through the hole in the base bead. Repeat the stack and go back down through the base bead, and so on. You can repeat as many times as you can pass through the hole in the base bead. In this case, the multiple small stacks form the anchor bead.

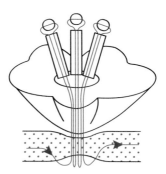

If you are securing a thick or large round bead, it is a good idea to use seed beads on each side of the bead for the return. This covers the thread up to the bead and down from the bead to the fabric, rather than drawing the fabric up to the level of the hole in the bead. Another way to anchor a large bead is to place it at an angle to the quilt top, adding enough beads to cover the thread.

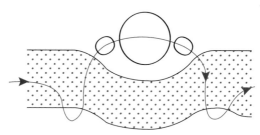

Returns for large bead

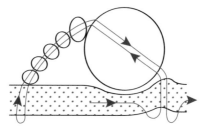

Pulled over at angle

Beads with a Hole through One Side or End

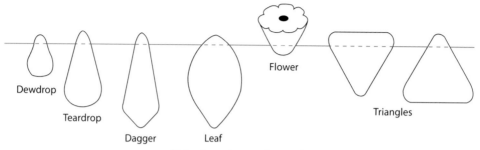

Holes through one side or end

Beads with a hole through one side or end are the most difficult beads to keep in place. They tend to rotate around the thread and are my last choice, unless the color or shape makes them irresistible, in which case I use them. This category includes dewdrops, raindrops, teardrops, lentils, dagger beads, some leaves and flowers, triangles with the hole parallel and close to one side or through one point, and so on. These are the most difficult shape and hole combinations and are to be used only when they are exactly the right shape or color or when no other alternative presents itself. I use what I call a chicken foot stitch to secure them.

1. Come up from the back (A) and pass through the bead. Go down immediately on the other side (B).

2. Come back up a little way from the first stitch (C) and pass back through the hole. Here is where you can finalize the position of the bead by pulling sideways in one direction or the other, thereby rotating the axis of the bead.

3. Go down (D) and come back up on the other side of the first stitch (E); then go through the hole again, going down to the back (F) to secure the stitch and then either coming back through the bead for the fourth time or continuing on to something else.

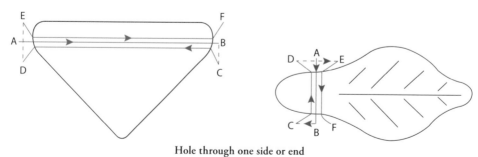

Hole through one side or end

Using Basic Stitches to Create Design Elements

Using Single or Seed Stitch

Single or seed stitch (page 34), with all its variations, is the large space filler. It creates a number of textures, quilts areas with the added advantage of a sprinkle of color, and makes subtle lines of dots and dashes that the eye can follow without having to make a long solid line. It's difficult to isolate a technique and intentionally use just one stitch, although the seed stitch does just that most easily. I came across a beautiful coffee table book of Australian Aboriginal art, and the pictures were beautiful in a strange way. They were constructed of dots and spaces filled with solid color and were very mystical in intent. What I envisioned was a whole series of small quilts in reverse appliqué with large or small beads as the dots. *Raven Dreaming* was the first piece I did in that style, and I used only the seed stitch—just single beads and two-bead stacks. It is quite amazing how one can change the color value of an area with a layer of dots of another color.

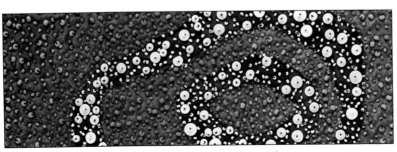

Detail of *Raven Dreaming* (page 97)

Adding Texture and Color

If you have a large bland area and you need to quilt it, single stitch does that nicely. You can add a variety of textures just with the stitch patterns you use between beads. Working back and forth in a zigzag pattern, you can pull up a ridge of fabric that forms a crack or crevice in the stone.

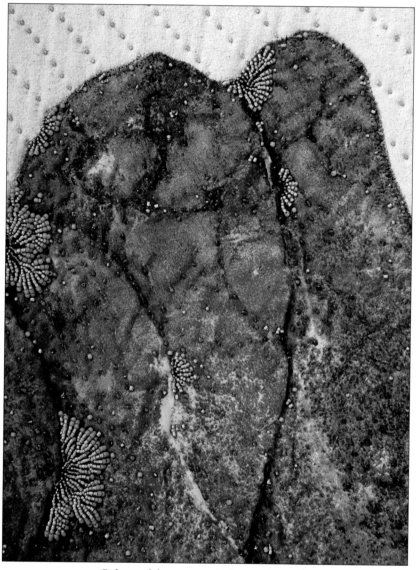

Ridges and dots on stone in *Serenity* (page 98)

You also can enhance the existing fabric's design, especially if you are using a print with lots of dots, by using beads of similar colors spread out over the surface. Create the texture of an orange rind with #15 seed beads, just a little darker orange than the orange fabric. Another possible use would be sprinkling white seed beads over the surface of a strawberry—color and texture at the same time!

Centered Squared is an example of using a large photograph printed on fabric. The finished piece is 52″ × 52″, which is a very large area to bead. I had the base design in the center and the seams machine quilted to keep the batting and backing from slipping around and to delineate the design. Working from the center out and leaving the central figure delineated only by the machine stitching outlining him, I beaded the flower that's radiating out from him with couched lines of mostly clear Iris bugles and seed beads. Then, I moved out into the starry sky behind, where I lightly sprinkled a variety of colors and shapes of seed beads and crystals. There were places where I wanted stitches to continue the quilting but no bead. It's really very simple to just take a stitch and move on to the next area where you want a bead. The hardest part is remembering not to pick up a bead on your needle.

NOTE

Spacing becomes crucial in covering large areas with single stitch. The eye tends to connect the dots, so keeping it random becomes a challenge, especially when you are working with a number of sizes and different colors of beads. I find that working back and forth in parallel lines with most of the beads in place and just a few off works well and covers the space rapidly.

The white banding around the eight-pointed star was more heavily stitched, with lots more color and a wide variety of sizes of beads, from #15 to #6 and with 4mm and 6mm crystals. I was trying to cover the space with quilting and discovered that I was making ridges as I tacked back and forth from edge to edge. I didn't want ridges, so from there on I tried to be careful not to work in zigzag lines unless I wanted ridges. Stitching large areas with a similar size and color of beads can become boring unless you find that almost Zen state in which your hands pick up beads and place them while part of your brain decides where to go next and which bead to use.

Dotted sky background in *Centered Squared* (page 90)

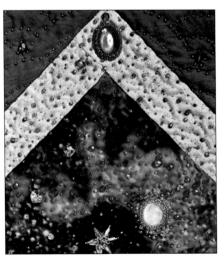

White bands in *Centered Squared*

Making Dotted Lines

There are times when you have a large space you wish to texture and quilt. If you want lines that are not solid but interrupted, you might use a series of dotted lines. The dots in the peach to lavender panels of *Centered Squared* were an exercise in using seed beads in a running stitch to quilt a large area with a traditional quilting pattern. I drew in the fan lines with a chalk pencil, using a stencil I created, so I could invert the pattern on each side of the points and have continuity of design throughout the whole band of fan shapes. I used a neutral-colored #11 seed bead slightly darker than the fabric to bead the areas.

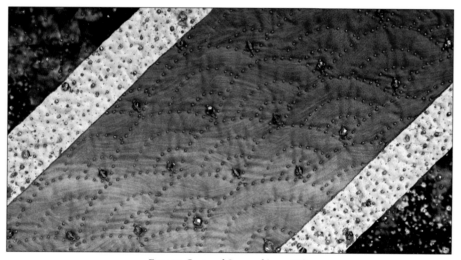

Fans in *Centered Squared* (page 90)

Later, I designed *Serenity* around the same technique of making dots of beads form lines. After placing the stones and beading them, I drew in the lines of raked gravel with a chalk pencil, using a yardstick to get the perspective correct and to make the lines continuous from the top left to the bottom right, behind the rocks.

Dotted lines forming furrows in raked gravel in *Serenity* (page 98)

Using Tall Stacks, Fringes, and Loops

The difference between a tall stack (page 35) and a strand of fringe (page 41) is a matter of semantics and the number of beads. The main difference is that the stack is intended to stand perpendicular to the surface. Fringe is intended to hang down parallel to the surface, keeping in mind that the traditional use of an art quilt is to hang on a wall. Tall stacks, or fringe, if you will, can be used to create the center of a flower or to raise a leaf above the surface of the quilt. The centers at right show a series of stacks topped with a larger anchor bead, with the bases of the stacks closer together than the tops have room for so they all radiate out from the center.

Center of *White Poppy*

Beaded bezel in *Time Is Flying* (page 94)

The fringe on a portion of *Smoke and Mirrors* was intended to look as if the panel of red silk were fraying at the bottom. Starting with strands of fringe at the bottom of the panel, I created more strands as I worked my way up the panel. I shortened the strands of fringe until they merged with the couched lines, so they appeared to grow out of the lines sewn to the surface.

You may want to make a large dense center for a flower or other raised dense area of beads. In the middle of the central poppy of *The Blue Miranda*, I wanted to raise the ring of purple stamens of the poppy and create a random, solid area of beads. I used loops going every which way. Most of the loops had a bugle bead, frequently not quite in the center of the loop, so the bead was not quite parallel with the surface.

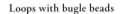

Loops with bugle beads

Fringe on left panel
of *Smoke and Mirrors* (page 96)

Center of poppy in *The Blue Miranda* (page 92)

Combining Back Stitch and Couching

Back stitch (page 36) and couching (page 37) both make lines, and I rarely use just one or the other. I'm not sure there is a right or wrong way to go about beading. Whatever works for you is your best way, and with practice, you'll find your own style. The technique is just a vehicle to put down beads where you want them and be sure they stay there. My style of beading tends to be very organic, moving back and forth from enhancing what is already in the fabric to putting in design elements not found there. Vines would be a good example of putting in elements not found in the fabric. They could be added over the rest of a piece to change the visual texture. When making vines with leaves, you might do a couched main stem and then go back and add little branches with the leaves using back stitch.

Vines with couching and back stitch in *Dogwood and Ivy*

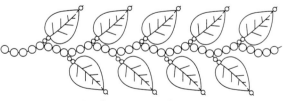

Bead arrangement for vine

I tend to use couching for long lines when I want to see where the line is going and be able to compose it as I go. I find it easier to make gentle curves with couching, keeping the flow of the line going, rather than breaking it up into a series of short lines. Back stitch is filler for me. It is what I do when I come to the end of a long line and only have a little way to go, or when I want a side branch or stem for a leaf to be tied into a main branch.

Branches in *Fall Study*

Branches in *My Father's Shadow* (page 99)

Another example can be found in the spiderweb in *At Risk*. Here the main support structure of the web was put in with a combination of couching and back stitch, and then the short lines were added between the main ones, primarily with back stitch.

Spiderweb from *At Risk* (page 100)

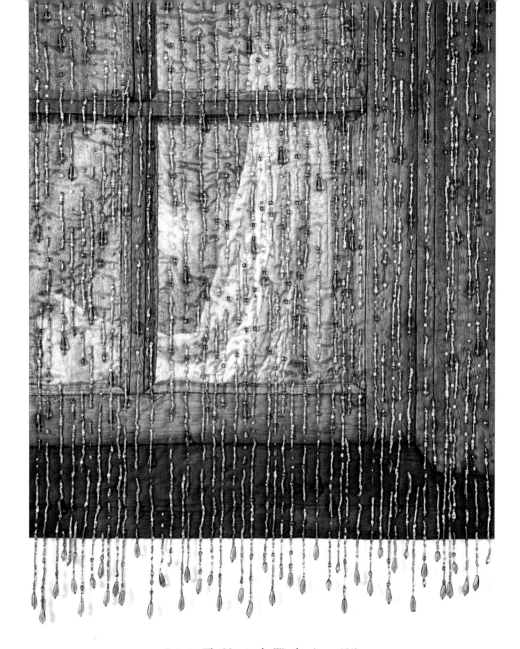

Rain in *The Man in the Window* (page 101)

Machine-Sewn Lines

Sometimes you want a clean, straight line of beads, either on a line already in the composition or as an added texture. Such was the case with *The Man in the Window*. I wanted the appearance of being outside, looking at a window while standing in the rain. This meant the rain needed to go over both the window frame and the panes of glass. I assembled the quilt top, added batting and backing, and then machine quilted the mullions of the window and the lines forming the frame. After that, I machine stitched in broken parallel lines over the whole piece, running them right up to the top and bottom edges. When I beaded the rain, I essentially beaded in-the-ditch, using short and long segments to suggest drops and streaks. When I had finished beading, stopping the stitching about ½″ from the approximate edge, I bound the edges and then finished the lines of beads out to the finished edges of the quilt. I added the fringe last, continuing the lines of rain right off the edge of the windowsill by starting the strand in the line sewn to the quilt and continuing down from the edge.

Multiple Parallel Lines

Multiple parallel lines can be used to create a heavier line than you would get from a single line of beads and are usually preferable to a lone line of big beads. (Sometimes even #6 beads are not thick enough to create the desired line; they do not make good lines because the tops and bottoms of the beads are often not parallel to each other.) If I were doing a tree trunk, I would start at one edge with a row of #8 beads and taper this first row by changing to #11 of the same color as I worked my way up the trunk. Then I would perhaps go to a row of #11, in the same color or a slightly different shade, and take that row further up the trunk. I would gradually taper the trunk by dropping a row or merging rows as I got closer to the top. I would continue the process until the trunk reached the appropriate thickness. As the rows are added, the lines of beads should be couched from the side of the line away from the previous line, toward the previous line. Occasionally, couching over both lines keeps them snuggled up to one another.

Tree trunks in *My Father's Shadow* (page 99)

Sometimes I may combine short parallel lines of beads with long perpendicular back stitched lines, as in the case of the birch tree trunks in *Reflections*. Here I started with white "fairy frost" fabric for the trunks; then I put the shadows and bark lines in with beads, giving them dimension and texture at the same time.

Tree trunks in *Reflections* (page 102)

Using Lazy Stitch

Augmenting Back Stitch and Couching

I mostly use this stitch to augment back stitch or couching. For example, in the dragon in *There Be Dragons Here*, I moved freely from back stitch to lazy stitch to couching and back to lazy stitch depending on the length of the line I was beading. In this case, all the information of the dragon's whiskers and claws was in the printed fabric already. All I had to do was modify some lines slightly and choose the size and color of the bead to cover them. I used lazy stitch (page 38) in the shortest lines, and when they got past five or six beads in length I would couch (page 37) or back stitch (page 36), depending on where I wanted to go next. Designs such as this are predicated on the availability of beads in a number of different sizes (usually #15, #11, and #8) that are all the same or similar color and finish.

Dragon in *There Be Dragons Here (page 67)*

Filling in Areas

Lazy stitch is most frequently used to fill in areas to give a dense texture or make broad lines. The ravens' wings and bodies in *The Ravens of Angel's Crest* are an example of filling in a fairly large area almost completely. Some of the lines are couched, but most of the bugle beads are laid in with a lazy stitch. The gloss and iridescence of the raven's plumage is suggested with a combination of plain black beads and beads with an AB (Aurora Borealis) finish.

Ravens in *The Ravens of Angel's Crest* (page 103)

Detail of *Cats* sampler

Creating Lines and Borders

Lazy stitch (page 38) can also be used to create thick lines for borders or to outline objects. The former is illustrated by a section of border in *Cats*, a small sampler I use as a demo for my Borders and Bezels class. The change in direction is effective, especially if one is easily bored, but be advised: You will find one direction of the angle easier to bead than the other. If the piece is small enough, you can turn it upside down and continue beading the border in the same way.

It is easier to keep the edges of the rows aligned if you baste or draw chalk guidelines before starting. I had to rip out whole sections of the crocodile outline several times and redraw them with chalk to get all the beads aligned perfectly on the crocodiles found on the borders of *Australian Dreamscape*.

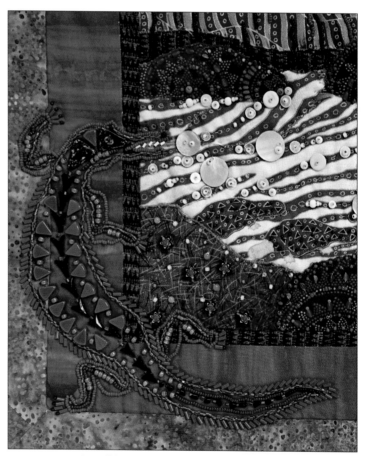

Crocodile in *Australian Dreamscape* (page 104)

Close-up of Australian fabric without beads

Combining Lazy Stitch and Couching

Australian Aboriginal Meets American Indian is a piece I designed for a demo of beaded bezels for the Road to California show in 2010. I did the soft-edge appliqué face using an Australian print, added batting and backing, and machine stitched the basic lines. I wanted to bead a little of the design before I started putting the mirrors in and found myself using a combination of couching (page 37) and lazy stitch (page 38). If you look closely, you will see which way the beads are lying on the thread and that the long thin lines are couched. The fatter lines, where the beads run perpendicular to the direction of the line, are done in lazy stitch. It was fast and fun to fill in the spaces.

Detail of *Australian Aboriginal Meets American Indian* (page 105)

Bits and Pieces

Beading on Quilts

I'm right-handed and usually bead horizontally from right to left or vertically, either toward or away from myself. This means turning the piece I'm working on. For a small piece, this is not a problem. When the top, batting, and backing are basted together, I start somewhere near the center and work out toward the edges, turning as I go to get the angle I need for the next stitch. However, when the piece is larger, turning can become problematic. I usually start in or near the center and use my left hand under the quilt to feel the needle to be sure the stitch goes all the way through to the back. Those of you who have done hand quilting will know what I'm talking about. In order to get your hand placed under the quilt, you may need to roll up the quilt around the area where you are working and pin it in place.

I also tend to work with my needle remaining on the surface rather than pushing the needle through to the back with one hand and then reaching under the quilt with the same hand to push it back through to the front. I've learned to judge where the needle has to come out to place the next bead and take the stitch with my dominant hand remaining on top. My left hand holds the fabric bunch and feels when the needle is through to the back. This means I may have four or more rolls of fabric surrounding the area where I am working. The larger the quilt, the larger the diameter of the rolls. For me, this tends to limit the size of the quilts I make, even with my large hands. One of the reasons I like the banner or scroll format is that the quilt can be rolled up at either or both ends and the center is still reachable from either side. I can then bead lines parallel to the long axis of the quilt, working toward the left. By rotating the entire quilt 180°, I can work from the center up toward the top and then down toward the bottom. I still work from the center in all four directions, keeping the quilt balanced, but there are only two rolls of fabric to deal with.

There Be Dragons Here, rolled to working area

Because the beading on a piece may be denser in some areas than others, the quilt may shrink unevenly and the original shape may become distorted, so leave an area of at least 1″–2″ from the raw edge unbeaded. When I've finished beading to this margin, I trim the quilt, squaring it up to the shape and size that I want the finished quilt. This leaves enough area so that when the binding is machine sewn on, beads will not be crushed in the seam. After the binding is sewn on, I finish beading, either to the edge of the quilt or to the binding and sometimes even over the binding. I use a number of binding methods, depending on the look I want. Sometimes I use the binding as a frame, and sometimes I turn the binding to the back so the design goes all the way out to the edge, like an unframed canvas.

Using Beads as a Design Element

When sewing beads onto a quilt, you have two basic choices: You can embellish your quilt, adding sparkle and color, or you can incorporate the beads into the design to create specific elements of the design. Both choices are valid. The techniques for sewing beads on fabric, and making them stay where you want them to, are essential for either choice.

Embellishment is a broad category that includes beads, sequins, yarn, lace, ribbon, Angelina fibers, and so on. It's fun and rewarding and can turn an ordinary quilt into a dazzler. This would be adding to the design, embellishing it. Most embellishment is added to a completed design to improve it. However, if you make a conscious choice to incorporate beads into a quilt, why not start with them as a major design element?

If you are using beads as part of a design based on fabric, you have three basic choices. You can enhance and add to what is already on the fabric, you can superimpose your design over the fabric with the beads, or you can combine enhancing with superimposing. This sounds complicated and all too much like what my friend Rosemary Eichorn calls "adult sewing." The choices are really made on a subconscious level, starting with a love of beads and a desire to use them on the quilt.

Partially finished *There Be Dragons Here*, **unrolled**

Using Beads to Enhance the Design

When you're thinking about a piece and have fabric that speaks to you, what are you going to do? Are there flowers that need to have beaded centers, cacti that need thorns, lines that need to be emphasized? As you go about realizing the design, you are augmenting what's already there in the fabric. I once had a bolt of fabric leap off the shelf into my arms, shouting, "Bead me! I'm an iguana!" I bought some yardage and took it home not knowing what I was going to do with it, except turn it into an iguana. I am familiar with iguanas from when I was stationed on the Navy base in Guantanamo Bay, Cuba. They are vegetarians, so I needed a habitat where my iguana might be found: Execute Project Jungle. Not easy when the greens available are not jungle greens. I settled for some caladium leaves and material texture resembling leaves and some fabric I could fussy cut leaves from. Next I found fabric that looked like woven wicker, and so on. The entire quilt started with and was based on a fabric that, when enhanced with beads, looked like iguana skin.

Iguana in *The Lotus Eater* (page 89)

Using Beads to Add a Design Element

In *The Man in the Window,* beads were used to add rain as an additional design element. The man and the window frame were created with fabric. The rain was added over the top of everything, telling the viewer that he or she is outside, standing in the rain, and looking into the room. I started the piece with an image of a man, a technique for making fabric look like old wood, and a desire to use rain to establish the environment for the viewer. The rain, added over the top of everything else, also created another layer or dimension.

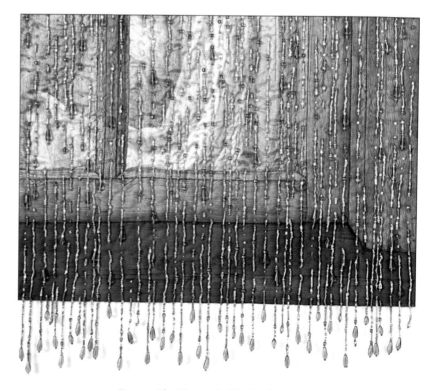

Rain in *The Man in the Window* (page 101)

Using Beads to Enhance and Add Design Elements

Most of my quilts are a combination of enhancement and addition. Sometimes the lines and shading are already in the fabric. Sometimes I add them, like the beaded lines in *Tenuous Membrane*. I used beads both to emphasize color, like the lines of turquoise blue beads, and to define shapes. Sometimes the lines just extend from or connect to a shape already there; sometimes, by outlining a shape, they further define that shape. If you look at the back of *Tenuous Membrane*, you will notice that most of the quilting has been done by machine. I used resin-bonded wool batting in this quilt, and I had it machine quilted to keep the back and the batting in place while I beaded the front. In this case I wanted the machine quilting to be visible, so a multi-colored thread of a complementary color was used. The machine quilting was almost entirely stitched in-the-ditch, so the design would show on the back. The hand quilting, worked in areas not having machine quilting, is done in a pale lavender thread so it disappears into the batik fabric. I didn't plan where to put each bead as much as let the design tell me where I needed more of one color or another—then the beads took over and told me where they wanted to go.

Back of *Tenuous Membrane* (page 11)

Go with the Flow

I have sometimes had students who seemed to overintellectualize the whole process; I usually suggest that they try to stop thinking and let their hands just do it. For me, working on a subconscious level seems to work best. I will have a general idea of what I want to do with the beads, and then I get lots of beads out and ready to use. I try to turn off my critical thinking process as much as I am able, and I let my eyes and hands do what they need and want to do. I don't choose to use a couching stitch or lazy stitch so much as see where the beads need to be and let my hands put them there. It becomes a very Zen thing, and if I can find it, I can stay in that state for several hours. Usually the phone rings, or I find that there is a world out there because I realize I'm hungry or need a pit stop, or my fingers and back have started to cramp. Then I lose the rhythm and have to find it all over again when I next pick up the piece.

Elements That Affect Beading

Time

Time is a design element. Is there a due date for the project? Will you have enough time to do the beading in the way you want to see it done, or will you have to modify the density or the type or size of bead used? Do you have all the beads you need, or will you need more time to round them up?

Availability

Availability is a design element. When designing, it's a good idea to take into account what's readily available in the way of materials. Dense beading and long lines of couching eat up beads and thread. So does fringe, big-time. Do you have enough beads in the right color, size, and finish? Do they even exist? Does that shape or color come in more than one size? Do you have as many leaves as your design calls for? Are they readily available, or are they vintage and not available anywhere anymore? Is it a handmade, one-of-a-kind bead? Can you order more from your source? The same goes for needles and thread.

Line

Line is a very important design element. How thick or thin; whether it's curved, straight, or jagged; whether it's hard-edged or soft—line characteristics are all important. A hard-edged, straight line moves at a different speed visually than a soft, curved line. Is it going to move your eye right out of the composition? How can you slow it down or bring it to another element in the design to keep the eye moving around the composition? All these are questions related to each individual design and can only be answered by the designer.

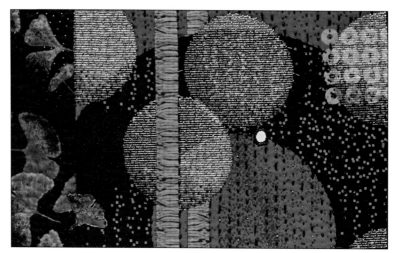

Notice that the straight and curved lines of the *Smoke and Mirrors* (pages 92 and 93) design are hard-edged, where the color contrasts with the color next to it and soft-edged where the color next to it blends more closely.

Color

Color, whether of beads, fabric, or thread, is another important design element. It's easier to design around a specific red bead if you have it, know it is available, or know where it can be obtained rather than to go looking for it because you really want that special red bead. Such a bead might not even exist in the size or finish you want. It is easier to start with a thread color that you have lots of (as long as it disappears on the back) than to have to stop because you've run out. And don't forget that beads, like fabric and yarn, are subject to great differences in color from lot to lot.

Texture

Many subtle textures can be created with beads, thread, fabric, and batting. Consider it a design element, too, because texture can lend visual reality to a shape just as much as shading can. Beads, depending on their size, color, and finish, and the way they are sewn on, can create a wide variety of textures. We've discussed many, and maybe, with what you've learned from this book, you can even invent many more textures of your own.

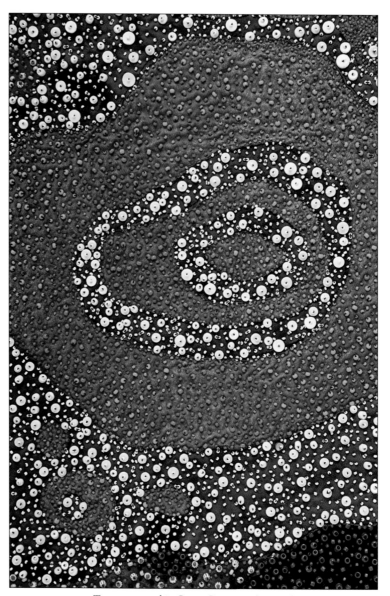

Texture created in *Raven Dreaming* (page 97)

Scale

Scale is also a design element. In order to make the grass in *My Father's Shadow* appear to recede up the hill, I had to keep it in proportion according to the laws of perspective. As it got further away, it had to get smaller. I went so far as to break bugle beads in half and file the sharp ends to have shorter bugles because the bugles I was using came only in one size. I also wanted the trees to appear real, so their leaves had to be in scale with the landscape. This limited and governed my choices.

Contrast

Contrast is another element that comes into play in designing a piece. When a design is too "blah," it may be because of lack of contrast. Contrast can include light and dark, bright colors played against grayed colors, large against small, or hard edges versus soft edges. Too much sameness causes the eye to stop wandering about the design and look somewhere else. The same could be said for too much contrast. The eye becomes weary and gives up because it is not able to adjust to the rapid change.

It takes a lifetime of study to find and learn to work in your own style. I'm still learning what beads will do when applied to quilts, and I haven't begun to learn all there is to know about ways to put elements together to produce the desired results.

Grass in *My Father's Shadow* (page 99)

Contrast of light and dark in *My Father's Shadow*

Frustration Levels and Time Crunches

Beading can be a rewarding and enriching experience. Beaded surfaces have a richness of texture that cannot be duplicated with machine stitching. But beading does require huge amounts of time. Working with materials that are fighting you, or within a time frame that is too short, is not a constructive use of your time. Because beading is a very time-consuming process, you will find that you have to allow yourself extra time to look through your stash and see what else might work, or to just sit and think about beads and think about what you are going to do next.

If you have to stop soon and go fix dinner, or get to an appointment downtown, don't rush and attempt to finish the next row, the thread, the next leaf, or whatever you're working on. You might have to rip it all out when you come back to it later.

Try to leave yourself open-ended time to work in. Beading, like hand sewing, always takes more time than it seems like it should. Unlike hand sewing, I find beading hard to put down and pick up again without some "think about what I'm doing" space. It takes me a while to get back into the rhythm of whatever piece I'm working on—and being male, I don't multitask well or switch gears rapidly.

Tangling Thread

If your thread keeps tangling, check to see if you are threading the end cut from the bobbin and knotting the other. If you are, reknot the thread at the other end. You'll find that some bobbins are wound backward. (Don't ask. I don't know how, but it's true.) If that doesn't work, throw the bobbin away and select another. Thread is probably the most inexpensive material you are working with. It's not worth the frustration.

Getting the Needle into Tiny Beads

Size #14 and #15 beads may seem awfully small when you first start using them. However, the holes are not much smaller than those of #11 beads. The thickness of the bead wall has been reduced to make the smaller size, not the diameter of the hole (much).

If you can't see them well enough to pick up beads with your needle, keep your beads in a pile and push the tip of the needle through the pile. Sooner or later you will have one or more beads on the needle. Or if a bead is lying hole side up and you can see the hole, lay the tip of the needle on the edge of the bead and gently push down. The bead will leap onto the needle—it's bead magic; trust me. These techniques work for other seed bead sizes as well.

If you are couching, keep your piles of beads tidy and just run the needle through many times to pick up a quantity of beads rapidly. Four or five passes will usually give you a straw needle's length of beads.

Gravity

Strange as it may seem, when you are using a great many beads on a quilt, gravity is also a design element to be considered. Art quilts are almost always hung on walls. This means the beads must be tied through to the back so the piece will hang well and the weight of the beads does not make the fabric sag or the quilt top pull forward and down. That may sound obvious, but it is something that has to be considered in the design. Any bead stacks, fringe, or loops will hang down unless otherwise secured to the surface. They might stand up nicely when you are working with them on a horizontal surface, but they will droop sooner or later when hung on a wall. This is not a disaster, just something to realize and plan for.

Whatever you create depends on what materials you have available and your imagination. Learn to believe in and trust in your imagination. Imagination and creativity are there within every one of us. We all have them, although some may have allowed them to atrophy, sent them into hiding, or suppressed them. Find them, woo them, and appreciate them in yourself and in others.

Bonus Feature—
Making a Beaded Bezel

What's a Bezel?

Frequently, you will come across a cabochon or shell that does not include a hole to sew through, a button with a broken shank or no holes, a mirror, or a "flat-back" that you want to attach to your quilt. Short of glue, the most satisfactory way I've found is to use a beaded bezel. What's a bezel, you ask? In a piece of jewelry, it is the metal band that holds stones, such as cabochons, in place. Its purpose is to hold the stone securely. What are cabochons? Unfaceted precious or semiprecious stones with flat backs are called cabochons, and for the sake of clarity, I'll refer to all such items as cabs. You can make a cage bezel with connected stacks, but I prefer the solid kind using back stitch to secure the bottom row of beads, and then I peyote stitch (see Second Row, page 77) the next three or more rows.

Various bezeled cabs in *Byzantine Bezels and Beads, Oh My!* (page 109)

Materials

- Quilt with the place for the bezeled cabochon marked in chalk

- Cabochon stone, shell, mirror, button, or anything with a flat back

- Double-sided adhesive tape on a roll at least 1″ wide (In my experience, Terrifically Tacky Tape is the only product strong enough to work in this application.)

- #11 seed beads to match or complement the stone

- #14 or #15 seed beads the same color as or a complementary color to the #11 beads

- Nymo D thread in a color similar to that of the beads or the quilt back

- #11 sharp or straw needle (unless the #15 seed beads have very small holes, in which case use a #12)

- Work scissors for trimming tape (Warning: Do not use good sewing scissors because the blades will get gummy and nasty.)

NOTE ─────

I especially like to use Czech seed beads since there is a great deal of irregularity in size and I will have thin beads to use in the top rows.

Applying the Tape

The first thing to do when creating a bezel is to secure the cabochon or shell firmly to the quilt top with Terrifically Tacky Tape, so it will not shift as the bezel beads are added.

1. Unroll a length of Terrifically Tacky Tape.

2. Hold a length in your hand, sticky side up, and place the cab, flat side down, on the tape.

If the tape is not wide enough to cover the cab from edge to edge, place the cab all the way to one edge of the tape. Piece 2 lengths of tape by butting the edges together rather than overlapping them. It doesn't matter if the tape does not quite meet on the interior seam as long as it goes all the way out to the edge of the stone.

3. Holding the cab flat side down, with the sticky side of the tape up, trim the tape as close to the edge as you can.

It is important to trim carefully, not allowing any tape to protrude beyond the edge of the cab. The first row of beads around the cab is sewn as close to the stone as possible. If your needle passes through the tape, the tip will get sticky and collect beads like a magnet the next time you go to pick up one. It's not a big deal; just clean off the needle tip by wiping it on a cloth or rub it with your fingers. However, it can be annoying enough to cause you to not want it to happen again.

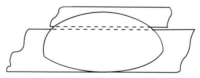

Apply tape to flat side of stone.

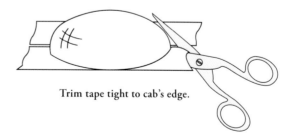

Trim tape tight to cab's edge.

If you are inclined to save the larger pieces of tape as you trim, I have found that sticking them back on the roll close to the cut edge works best. I tried sticking them to the plastic bag I keep the roll in, but when I went to pull the pieces off, just the plastic cover came off. The pieces had permanently adhered themselves to the bag.

4. Peel off the sheet of plastic covering the other sticky side of the tape and apply the cab to the quilt, being very careful to place it exactly where you want it. (I like to use a pair of blunt tweezers.) You can only reposition it once or twice before the sticky side is too coated with fuzz to hold well. Should this happen, do not despair. Pull off the old tape and replace it with new.

Beading the Bezel

1. For a 1″ × 1½″ diameter cab, cut about a yard of thread.

You do not want to have to splice in a second piece of thread, so err on the side of a too-long piece to start with.

2. Stretch the thread well (page 29) before cutting. With a needle threaded with a single knotted thread, bury the knot and come up from the back next to the cab.

3. Mark the starting point on the fabric in some way or choose a point on the stone that is memorable. You will want to refer to this point later.

First Row

1. Working only with the fattest beads, pick up 4 beads with the needle. Snug the beads down to the quilt alongside the cab, and enter the quilt at the end of the row of 4 beads. Go through to the back. Come back up between the second and third beads, as close to the cab as possible, and pass through beads 3 and 4.

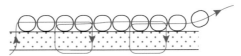

Four-bead back stitch

NOTE

As you poke through your pile of beads looking for the fat ones, set aside any thin ones you find. You will use them later, so put them in an easily available place. Sometimes you have to get beads on the needle to see which ones are thicker. They all look alike at first. Keep looking; there will be some difference.

2. Repeat Step 1 and continue on around the cab to finish the row, using only the fat beads. Try to complete the circle with an even number of beads (see left Note, page 77).

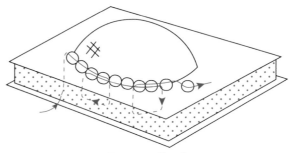

First row of bezel

3. Pass through where you started the row and continue on around through all the beads, coming out 1 bead past the marked starting point. That will reinforce the row, which is the base for the bezel and evens out the spacing, pulling the beads up against the cab.

NOTE

The even number is important because you will be using the peyote stitch from now on, and it works more easily with even numbers. If you do use an odd number, you will be working with a spiral instead of rows of beads. This will not be a problem, although it does cause an anomaly in the last row.

When you get to the space at the end of the row, do not be tempted to squash in four beads if there isn't really enough space. More space between beads on the bottom row of beads is preferable to not enough. Use two beads instead of four, or if the space won't quite accommodate two beads, go straight on through the beads you first laid down. The spaces between the beads will even out in the second row.

This is where a bezel can go very wrong and turn into a ruffle. If you have squished the beads too closely together, or used some or all skinny beads (note my highly technical verbs and adjectives) and then used fat beads in the next rows, the circumference will widen rather than contract. If this happens, remove the beads down to where the squeeze happened, or to where you've used thin beads, and start over.

FYI: While a back stitch is used for the first row of beads in a bezel, the process used for the second row (and any subsequent rows) is a peyote stitch.

Second Row

Pick up a bead on your needle, skip a bead, and insert your needle through the next bead. Pick up another bead on your needle, skip 1 base bead, and insert your needle through the next base bead. Continue doing this all the way around the circle, pulling the thread tight as you go.

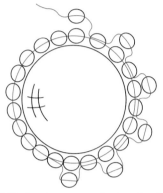

Add a bead on every other base bead.

My mantra for this is "pick up a bead, skip a bead, pass through a bead," continued to the end of the new row. You are basically putting a bead on top of every other bead. The beads will be hanging out and not look very tidy. Not to worry—they're supposed to look that way. You'll tidy them up with the application of the next row.

NOTE

Be careful not to exit a bead, pick up a bead, and go back into the bottom row in the same space. This will add a bead to the new row, and the last thing you want to do is add beads. You can check by inserting the tip of the needle in each new bead and pulling it away slightly from the bottom row. If the thread exits one bead in the bottom row and skips a bead to enter the next bead, it's correct. If it doesn't, you're in trouble; it's the easiest mistake to make, however. The only way to fix it is to pull it out and start over at that point. I'd like to add that I still do this every now and then. Everybody does. So if it happens, you will have lots of company.

Third Row

1. Go through the last bead in the bottom row, come up, and go through the first bead in the second row.

This is your "step up" to start the third row. If you do not have an even number of beads in the base row, you will not have a step up and will be doing a spiral. This is okay and will only cause a slight anomaly in the last row, where you have 2 #15 beads next to one another. It can be confusing, though, so it is best avoided by having an even count in the base row.

2. Add a bead and go through the next bead in the second row. Continue around the cab, adding a bead and passing through the next bead in the second row until you have completed that row, keeping the thread tension fairly tight and pulling the beads up against the side of the cab.

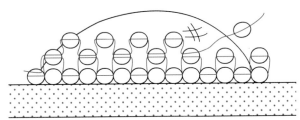

Add bead between second-row beads.

3. When you finish the third row, pass through the first bead in that row, the "up" bead, and pull the thread tight, so all the beads are lying close to the surface of the cab.

NOTE

Important: Keep the third row pulled tight against the cab.

It will look like you have two rows instead of three. If you look carefully, the second and third rows combine in one row that has the appearance of an "up" and a "down" bead. This is important to be able to see, because from here on you will be passing through the "up" bead and adding a bead on top of the "down" bead. If it helps you in the process, use my mantra for this row and future rows: "pass through a bead, add a bead, pass through a bead, add a bead," and so on. This is the easiest and fastest row. Enjoy it while it lasts. Depending on the size of the cab, you may need another row or two before you add the final row of #14 or #15 beads to pull in the top of the bezel.

The side of the cab, called the hip, may begin curving immediately. It may rise vertically for a time before starting the curve. The way it curves and the arc of the curve will determine the number of rows needed to hold the stone in place on the fabric. If it begins to curve inward immediately, you may need only two more rows. If the side goes straight up and then curves in, you will have to go past the point at which it begins to curve before starting to use skinny or smaller beads, interspersed among the regular-size beads, to reduce the circumference of the bezel.

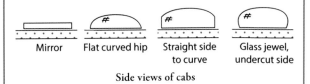

Mirror   Flat curved hip   Straight side   Glass jewel,
                               to curve   undercut side

Side views of cabs

Fourth Row and Onward to the Finish

1. Pick up a bead on the needle and continue the following rows with the same "pass through a bead, add a bead" technique, remembering to "step up" to the next row and keep pulling the rows tight against the cab. (If you are doing a spiral, because of an odd number of beads in the base row, you don't have a step up.)

Keep track of the rows by referring to the mark you made on the fabric at the beginning of the base row. When you are far enough past the inward curve of the cab that the bezel will hold the stone in place securely, change to all skinny beads or #14 or #15 beads. This will pull in the top of the bezel faster and help hold the stone tight. Here is where the anomaly of the "odd verses even" count of the first row shows up. At the end of the row you will have 2 #15 beads next to each other. It will only show if there is a distinct difference between the #11 and the #15. The "man riding by on a horse" rule applies here. (If a man riding by on a horse looks at the bezel, will he notice, especially if he's at a full gallop?)

When you've completed the final row with the #15 beads, pull it tight. You should not be able to pull the bezel away from or down the side of the stone. If it is still not tight enough, you may need another row of #15 beads.

2. After pulling the thread tight, hold the thread down to the cab with your left thumb while going through all the up and down beads (the last 2 rows), thereby reinforcing the top row.

This keeps the tension tight and allows you to pull the beads tight to the cab. I find that by maneuvering the needle, I can pass through 4 to 6 beads at a time. You may be able to go through only 2 at a time, but work your way around the inner edge of the bezel until you reach the beginning of the reinforced row. You will most likely not be able to do another row of reinforcement because of the size of the #15 holes.

3. Work your way down at an angle through the beads to the fabric and go through to the back. Tie off the thread and bury the end, or knot securely and continue beading. Your cab is now secure with a beautiful bezel!

Abalone shell bezels in *Laurel's Mermaid* (page 107)

Bezels for Mirrors

When making a beaded bezel for a mirror, the first steps are the same as for making a beaded bezel (page 74).

1. Cover the back of the mirror with the Terrifically Tacky Tape, and carefully trim the edges of the tape. Place the mirror in position on the quilt, and apply the first row, 4 beads at a time, with back stitch.

2. The second row of #11 seed beads is done the same way as on a regular bezel: "Go through a bead, pick up a bead, skip a bead, go through a bead," and so on.

Notice that if you have used #11 seed beads for the base row, they are approximately the same diameter as the mirror is thick. Therefore, the beads in the second and third rows can be pulled up onto the mirror's surface.

3. Go directly to #15 seed beads with the third row, where you are adding a bead between every bead. Your

mantra this time is "go through a bead, add a bead, go through a bead, add a bead," and so on.

4. Reinforce the second and third rows, which look like one row except every other bead is smaller, and then pull the thread tight. When you pass through the rows to reinforce them, you are most likely passing through the thread itself, and this helps further lock the beads in place.

5. After reinforcing, work the needle back down to the back and knot the thread.

You can use this same technique for button blanks (pieces of abalone or shell that have been cut into button shapes but not drilled) or any other thin, flat object that has no holes.

Bezeled bone faces and mirrors in *Death Touches Us All* (page 108)

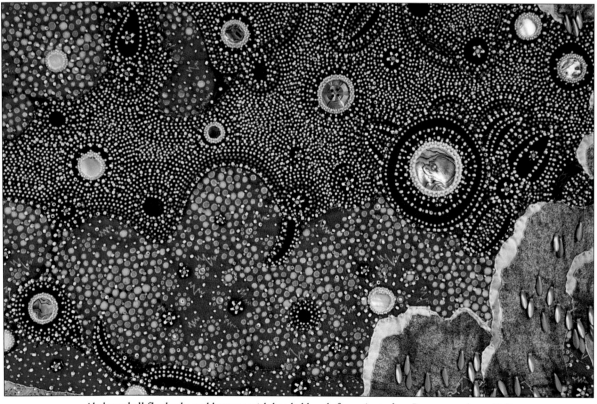

Abalone shell flat backs and buttons with beaded bezels from *Australian Dreamscape* (page 104)

Gallery

Detail of
Global Warming

Global Warming,
2008, 18″ × 52″

Fire and Ice,
2008, 18″ × 52″

Detail of *Fire and Ice*

After the Rains,
2004, 38″ × 46″

Detail of
After the Rains

Detail of
The Lotus Eater

The Lotus Eater,
2003, 31½″ × 37″

Centered Squared,
2010, 52″ × 52″

Detail of
Centered Squared

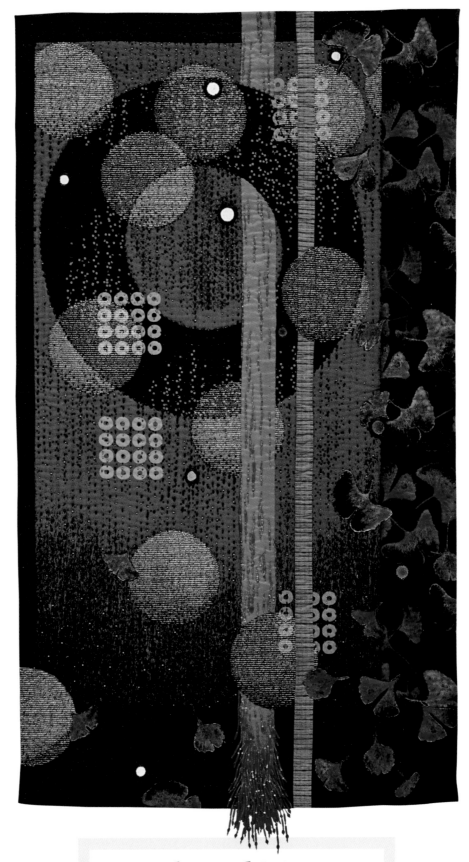

Smoke and Mirrors
(left panel), 2005, 29″ × 50″

Smoke and Mirrors
(right panel), 2005, 22½″ × 50″

Time Is Flying,
2007, 9″ × 13″

Detail of
Time Is Flying

The Blue Miranda,
2005, 23″ × 23″

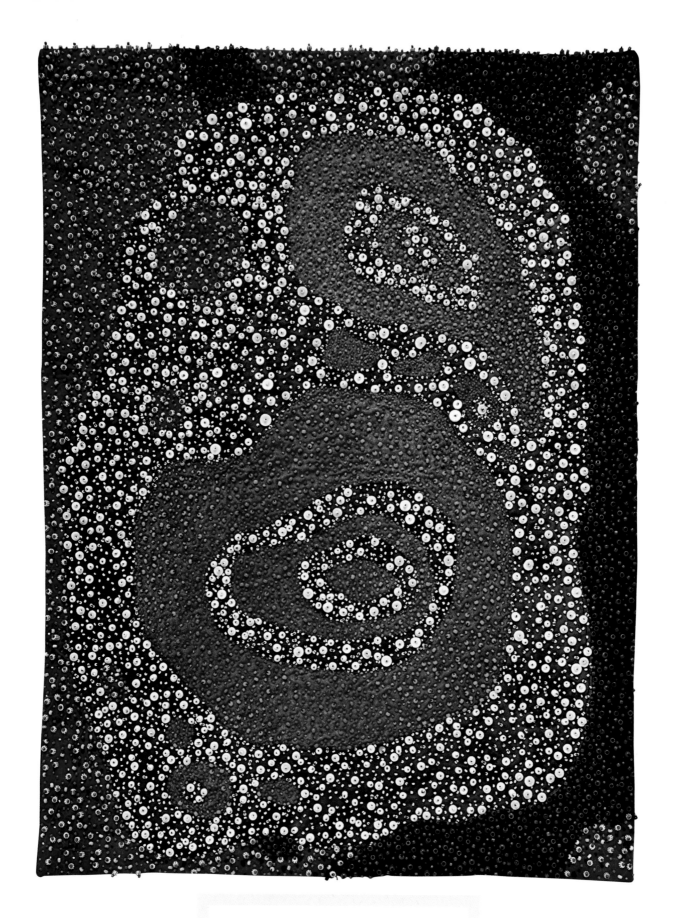

Raven Dreaming,
2009, 16″ × 21″

Serenity,
2011, 21½″ × 66″

My Father's Shadow,
2007, 44½″ × 36½″

At Risk,
2004, 39″ × 44″

The Man in the Window,
2009, 31″ × 32¾″

Reflections,
2006, 17½″ × 21½″

The Ravens of Angel's Crest,
2009, 35″ × 51½″

Australian Dreamscape,
2005, 42″ × 34″

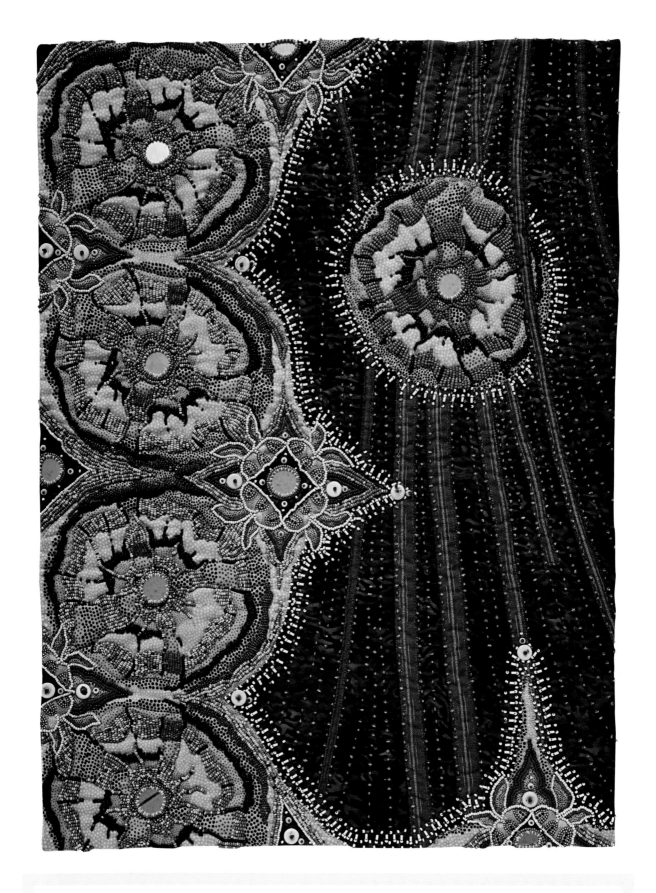

Australian Aboriginal Meets American Indian,
2011, 15″ × 20½″

Partial Eclipse,
2010, 18″ × 50″

Laurel's Mermaid,
2007, 10″ × 17″

Death Touches Us All,
2007, 27″ × 34″

Byzantine Borders and Bezels, Oh My!
2007, 21″ × 39″

Toco Toucan's Berries,
2011, 48″ × 84″

About the Author

Thom Atkins has been making things all his life. Somewhere there is a photograph of him at about three years old, decorating a mud pie with flowers and bits of sticks and shell. How things go together has always fascinated him. He came from a family where artistic expression was encouraged. Thom's grandmother taught him and his sister how to sew on a treadle sewing machine.

After graduating from San Jose State College with a Bachelor's of Art in interior decoration, he joined the Navy, where he went from the medical corps to medical illustration school, but the only illustration he did was in conjunction with the Smithsonian Institute, doing illustrations of the mammals of Vietnam. After leaving the Navy, he managed Friends of the Crafts gallery in Seattle. Still having the desire to make things, he took an extension class at the University of Washington on making stained glass.

Some 30 years ago, his sister, Robin Atkins, taught him the basics of bead embroidery on fabric. He's been fascinated with beads ever since, but sewing beads onto fabric and making stained glass didn't produce a decent living. He was also tired of the fragility of glass, so he went back to college, where he learned about welding, forging, silversmithing, and bronze casting. Bronze casting gave him back the tactile surfaces and the subtleties of three-dimensional curves and negative space.

A car accident terminated his career in sculpting in bronze. While recovering from the surgery to repair his wrists and thumbs, he thought about sewing beads onto cloth in such a way that the beads and the fabric both had a say in the design. He's been working with the delicate balance between beads and fabric in his designs ever since.

Thom and his wife live in Santa Cruz, California.

Great Titles *from* C&T PUBLISHING

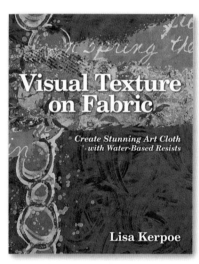

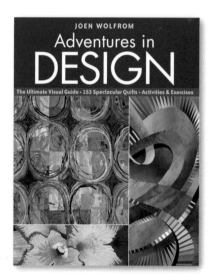

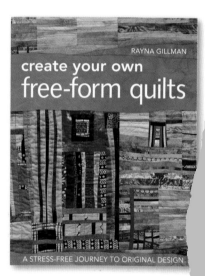

Available at your local retailer or **www.ctpub.com** *or* **800-284-1114**

For a list of other fine books from C&T Publishing, visit our website to view our catalog online.

C&T PUBLISHING, INC.
P.O. Box 1456
Lafayette, CA 94549
800-284-1114

Email: ctinfo@ctpub.com
Website: www.ctpub.com

C&T Publishing's professional photography services are now available to the public. Visit us at www.ctmediaservices.com.

Tips and Techniques can be found at www.ctpub.com > Consumer Resources > Quiltmaking Basics: Tips & Techniques for Quiltmaking & More

For quilting supplies:

COTTON PATCH
1025 Brown Ave.
Lafayette, CA 94549
Store: 925-284-1177
Mail order: 925-283-7883

Email: CottonPa@aol.com
Website: www.quiltusa.com

Note: Fabrics shown may not be currently available, as fabric manufacturers keep most fabrics in print for only a short time.